letting love in

How God Renews Relationships By Crushing Your Inner Critic

LINDSAY
MORGAN SNYDER

RHYDDID CREATIVE

LETTING LOVE IN:
HOW GOD RENEWS RELATIONSHIPS
BY CRUSHING YOUR INNER CRITIC

By Lindsay Morgan Snyder

Please direct inquiries about this book to:
lindsaysnyder.com

Names and non-essential elements in this book have been changed to protect the privacy of those involved.

Scripture quotations taken from the New American Standard Bible® (NASB) Copyright © 1960, 1962, 1963, 1968, 1971, 1972, 1973, 1975, 1977, 1995 by The Lockman Foundation. Used by permission. www.Lockman.org

Cover Design: Hope River Arts

Cover Images and Author Photo by:
Emily Wall Co.

Edited by: Karla Dial

ISBN 13: 978-1720401339
ISBN 10: 1720401330

To My Beloved

My beloved responded and said unto me, "Arise, my darling, my beautiful one, and come along!"
(Song of Songs 2:10)

Contents

Dedication

I dedicate this book to my nieces, those who call me Aunt Lindsay and my godchildren. I want you to know you were born to be the unique masterpiece Father God made. I never want you to settle for less than the Love of Jesus, the adoration of Father God and the Joy found in the Holy Spirit.

You're Incredibly Loved.
Be wild for Jesus.

Acknowledgments

Father God, Jesus, and Holy Spirit, you are my favorites, hands down.

My Book Doula, Ash! She has been with me the entire 3 years (of writing this book) listening to my crazy voice texts and reviewing my 2,000 different title/subtitle combinations. Thanks for staying with me Ash. The book wouldn't have been born without you.

My Secret Mentor, my fellow greeter at church who I later found out was not only an author of over 20 books but an award winning screenwriter. Your help, encouragement, time, and love is unprecedented. You never know who you might meet serving the Lord.

My friends that I would inundate with text messages and with questions of which title, which subtitle. Those of you heroes that read chapters and gave feedback even when it freaked me out.

Those of you who prayed when I thought I was losing my marbles. Thank you for the lessons about life and the Lord that came out in this book. You know who you are. From Atlanta to Los Angeles to Redding. I love you all.

My Family, thank you!

My sister, who is always sending back edits of whatever 'writing rendezvous' I find myself on.

My Mom and Dad, for allowing me to be me even if you often didn't understand what on earth I was doing.

My grandmothers, who I am pretty sure are my biggest fans.

The rest of my family, who would cheer me on from afar even if I were building cardboard boxes.

Love you all!

*You are more beautiful
than you realize!*

1

The Lies and the Love

Am I pretty enough? Am I good enough?

I was on a date, four vodkas in, consumed with worry, wondering what the guy across the table really thought about me.

Is he going to find someone better?

Am I worthy of a nice guy?

I couldn't stop the anxious thoughts from swirling around inside my head. Not even long enough to take a bite of my eggplant parmesan. The thoughts were so loud, the only relief I could find was more vodka.

"Lindsay, are *you* pretty enough?" asked the snarky voice in my head. "Not even close. Are you good enough? Ha, you know the answer to *that* one."

Hatred filled every word.

"Could he find someone better? *Hell-o-o-o-o*, Lindsay, just look around. Everyone is better than you. You're so stupid.

"You are worthless, Lindsay, disgusting."

The conversation at the table continued, but the conversation in my head overpowered it.

"Hey, Lindsay, what do you think?" my date asked. He had a stellar smile, a warm personality, and sort of a blurry face (or maybe that was the vodka). I raised my glass for another sip.

"Lindsay, Lindsay!" The mean voice clamored for my attention. "He would never like you; you aren't pretty enough."

I was so distracted I couldn't even process what my date was saying. All I could see was the waiter passing by. I signaled him with a wave— "Ah yes, thank you!"—to let him know I needed another drink.

I tried to ignore the mean voice in my head and listen to my date, but it was all I could hear. Worse yet, I agreed with it—to the point *it* felt like my own thoughts.

Lindsay, you are so worthless. This guy would never like you. Who are you kidding? No one will ever love you.

My poor date didn't stand a chance against the competition in my head. As I sat there agreeing with everything the mean voice was telling me, like how this guy would never like me, I got mad—and decided to ditch my date before he ditched me.

Liar, Liar, Liar

I wish I had known I was being lied to. I didn't realize my date probably really did like me. I couldn't see why someone else would like me when I didn't even like myself.

It would take me years to realize the root of my worry in this situation was rejection.

About a year later, the mean voice returned with a vengeance, kicking me while I was already down. I lay in my bedroom, heartbroken once again by a different failed relationship. I was crying so hard I could barely breath, feeling utterly rejected. My worry, my fear, had come true—again.

Lindsay, you are such a loser. See, you are so worthless. You might as well call it quits. You are ugly and disgusting, and no one will ever love you. Get used to it.

I felt as though some unseen force was beating me over the head with a crowbar—yet, strangely, it seemed to be coming from within. Alone and desperate, I had nowhere to turn. In agony, I muttered the word "God."

Now, I didn't believe in God at the time. It just came out of my mouth.

My sister believed in God and I always figured I could get into Heaven by giving her name at the door.

As if I were convincing some bouncer at club. I'd obviously spent way too much time in clubs.

Back To The Mean Voice

I had no context for this kind of fight, this mean voice that tormented me for decades. I thought it was me, I thought it was my own thoughts. But in a moment of deep despair and extreme emotional pain, I heard the God I didn't even believe in say:

"Lindsay, I am right here. I have always been right here."

And the mean voice went silent.

A tangible peace I had never known came over the room. It was thick, like a warm, snuggly blanket on a cold winter day.

And for the first time ever in my life I had a real encounter with a living God—the One I had thought was just a fairy tale for the past 29 years.

Fairy Tales

Fairy tales were not something I ever believed in; in fact, I loathed them. I thought they were ridiculous and stupid.

That was, until my Knight in Shining Armor showed up on a white horse, picked me up, and carried me away to a palace—and process. A process with a promise attached to it: a promise that He would be with me to hug me and bless me and talk to me when I was hurting. A big, beautiful promise that Love Himself would come in many forms in my process. He was the sweetest "man" I ever met, He knew me like no one else, and He loved me more than anyone.

He was kind and He was gentle. He knew my heart because He created it.

Love Stories Made Me Gag!

It's true, so I understand if they make you gag too. I personally hated them. I would often look at people that loved *Love Stories* as weak, naïve, and needy, silly to believe in such a "fairytale". I was sure they were made up to disappoint us.

That was, until I ran smack-dab into Love Himself and found He was more real than anything I had experienced on earth.

I stood corrected, Love was real. Love was a person! How did I miss this all these years?

I didn't think I wanted love, I thought I was just fine by myself, but the truth was deep down I was dying for it and little did I ever guess that God was Love.

I never knew God was strong, ready to defend me at any cost.

I never knew He was the Love that was going to untangle the lies that kept me bound; I had no idea He was the Love that was determined to set me free. He was the Love that wouldn't stand for the adversary of Fear wreaking any more havoc in my life. He was the Love that didn't care what it cost, the Love that was going to show me the battle He won for me centuries ago.

Me free from all that entangled me, finally. And with such an epic love story that only Love could write.

Love was committed to restoration and redemption. He was not worried about what anyone around me thought.

He did it for me. And Beloved, He will do it for you.

He lavished me with things that weren't "possible or normal." He did it in the middle of my pain. He did it in the middle of my confusion. It was Him who fought for my heart, long ago, long before I ever knew Him.

He promised He would never leave me or forsake me and He hasn't. He shocked me and surprised me—even spoiled me—in the midst of my pain.

He said He would never let me settle. He said He would help me overcome my fears of men, marriage, and dating.

He taught me to reposition my crown. See, He didn't cause my singleness. He first wanted me to understand what I was worth. He crushed the lies of the enemy in such an epic way.

He Is So For You

Love rescued me and Beloved, He will rescue you, too. That is who He is and that is what He does.

He wants what is best for us and He won't settle for less. He wants to fulfill our deepest desires—and those desires He knows how to uncover fully.

Will you let Him help you?

It is His greatest pleasure to untangle all that the world has put on you so you can receive all He has done for you.

He is a proud Daddy and a valiant Warrior who is on your side.

Let's look at the lies that hold us back, shed the layers, and position ourselves for pursuit. The pursuit of a lifetime, on earth as it is in Heaven.

This was a ten-year process for me, but the secrets I've learned are going to be revealed in the chapters ahead. Secrets that will make your process easier than mine! This is the goal: to reveal what took me a decade to learn so you can go further, faster.

So join me as we embark on the process to our promise. Let the fairy tale begin—the one we never thought possible, even the one we used to despise.

Let's journey through this thing called Love with Love Himself by our side, the Counselor and the Comforter of our soul.

• • •

2

The Lie of Worry

The words on the pages of my journal were riddled with anxiety, filled with self-condemnation, and disdain. I was worried, wondering frantically if I had done the "right thing" once again. Trapped in my own mind, I was unable to move through my own thoughts.

I felt as though there was no way out.

This time He won't come through, I thought to myself. *This time it's up to me; He has done enough.*

I had zero grace for myself and little trust in my God. Deep down, I knew God loved me—yet I didn't know His actual faithfulness. I feared everything was really up to me and I would screw it all up and ruin my life—which was quite an extreme thought for the situation at hand.

I felt completely unworthy of anything good. I questioned myself at every step. My thought life was a complete disaster.

What's Fear Got to Do with It?

Fear has a way of hiding itself deep within our souls—going unnoticed for decades, masquerading as us, lying, and saying that this is just who we are. *There is something deeply wrong with me,* we think.

I wonder what it is.

I'd try to put words to it, but the swirl would start. I would end up confused once again, wondering what on earth was wrong with me.

Lindsay, no one cares.

This is how it is.

This is who you are.

There's no way out, my worried mind would murmur.

But then a kind voice would suddenly interrupt and say, "Moment by moment, Lindsay. Walk with Me moment by moment, and I will show you."

The Father's Love

God is a loving, patient, and kind Father—and He was going to walk me through this process step by step.

I had to hold tightly onto His hand. I knew if I was going to overcome my debilitating insecurity when it came to men, dating and marriage, it would take an act of the miracle-working God.

I knew it, He knew it, my friends knew it—and heck, all the angels in Heaven knew it, too.

I would need to look to Him at every turn, or I wouldn't make it.

Starting at The Root

God kindly took my hand and led me moment by moment to the truth that *fear which causes worry is not from Him.*

I started to see worry as a bigger deal than society likes to tell us it is, mainly because it comes to kill, steal and destroy.

The thing about worry is, it feels normal.

I wonder if I am pretty enough?
That's worry.

I wonder if he likes me?
That's worry.
What if he doesn't choose me?
That's worry.
What if I get hurt?
That's worry.
What will other people think?
That's worry.

Worry is a thief. It will steal from you anything it can—your peace, your joy, your security, even your health. Just as we wouldn't allow a thief into our home to take whatever he wanted, we must not allow the thief of worry into our mind to steal from us, either.

Worry Has Stolen Enough

I don't know if you have ever felt tormented by worry, by the questions in your head—questions like, "Am I lovable?"

But these questions are set up to take us out, and they must be dealt with diligently.

I thought these questions were just a normal part of my personality. But after decades of believing lies that kept me stressed out and on guard, protecting myself even from good things, I realized this was not okay.

Feeling completely unworthy of anything good in life was my norm. I felt such distain for myself that I couldn't receive good things.

I couldn't receive love.

I didn't know my inability to receive love was at the root of my worried mind.

So Where Do We Start?

Worry, who are you? I wondered.

So, like any good word nerd, I looked up *worry* on a dictionary app—and was a little surprised by what I found.

The definition said, "to choke or strangle, to harass by tearing, biting or snapping, especially at the throat."

I took a screenshot of the definition after double-checking that I'd actually typed in the word "worry"—because that was not what I was expecting.

I thought it would say something like, "a condition all humans struggle with." But it didn't say that. It said "to choke or to strangle." I noticed not all dictionaries defined the word *worry* this way, so I dug a little deeper to find its origin. The English word "worry" comes from the Old English word "wyrgan" and Old High German word "wurgen"—both meaning "to strangle, to choke."

With a screenshot of my newfound intel in hand, I couldn't help but think how someone, at some point, had decided to normalize this tormenting word.

My screenshot said worry meant: "to disturb something repeatedly, to assail with rough or aggressive attack or treatment: to torment."

To torment?

I always thought worrying about someone was a kind gesture. Like "Hey, I worry about you. That means I love you because I think of you often."

But no, that is not what it said. It said "to torment."

And torment is not a kind gesture.

Jesus talks about the "tormentor" (referring to the enemy) in Scripture. He says:

"The thief comes only to steal and kill and destroy; I came that they may have life, and have it abundantly" (John 10:10).

When I think about my times of extreme worry in life—wondering if I was good enough, curious if I was worthy—I realized it absolutely stole my joy, destroyed my peace, and killed my hope. I realized by worrying, we are basically letting ourselves be tormented.

I knew what the Bible said in Philippians 4:6: *"Be anxious [worried] for nothing" (including dating, men or marriage—that's the LMS Version), "but in everything by prayer and supplication with thanksgiving let your requests be known to God"* and He will provide peace.

Ah, peace, yes—that is what we want.

Thirty-Seven Years of Worrying and It's That Simple?

Worry over and over again asked me the same question. "Lindsay, do you think he would really like you?" And worry wasn't just questioning me about men, it was questioning me about everything and it was tormenting.

What's the deal with this "worry," and how does it have the power to cause the world to torment itself?

So, like any good over thinker, I decided to ask Google—because Google knows everything, right?

To my surprise, the top answer in my Google search said the opposite of worry is "peace and confidence."

But how did World Wide Web suggest we get to this place of peace and confidence? It clearly wasn't referring to the peace and confidence that is found in Jesus Christ.

A few results down, I saw another answer: "The opposite of worry is *non-worry*."

Thanks Google. What on earth is non-worry? How do we just non-torment ourselves?

It's not that easy, Google! I wanted to scream.

A few results later I read that "worry is the opposite of faith"—which was interesting because it wasn't referring to faith in Jesus. It just said "faith." So I thought, *what do they mean by faith?*

The site described faith as "a belief in something for which there is no proof, complete trust."

According to Google, "worry" (to torment) is the opposite of faith. And also according to Google, faith means to trust.

Let's pause and read that again.

Worry—which means to torment (or be tormented)—is the opposite of faith, and faith means to trust.

But trust in what?

And then I was reminded that I don't have to figure everything out or "fix myself" because Jesus died on the cross for all of that.

Thanks, God.

It's best to let the Lord lead the fight. His burden is light and easy. We are to come to Him, and He will give us rest and show us the way out of our worried mind.

Now, let's take a moment to reflect.

Journal Moment

Grab your journal and let's ask Jesus a few questions.

Write "Me:" and then ask Him about whatever is on your heart. For example:

Me: Jesus, why do I worry about being rejected?

Then write "Jesus:" and listen to what He might be saying.

Jesus: Because, Honey, you are afraid it will hurt so much you won't recover.

Okay, it's your turn again. It's a conversation.

Me: Is that true, Lord?

Jesus: What do you think, Beautiful?

Me: It feels real, Jesus.

Jesus: I know, but is it true?

Me: I mean, probably not. But what am I supposed to do?

Jesus: About what?

Me: About my fear.

Jesus: What do you think you should do?

Me: I don't know.

Jesus: What are you asking, Lindsay? What do you really want to know?

Me: Am I going to be okay?

Jesus: Yes, Beautiful, you are.

I am not proposing any kind of simple formula here. I don't believe there is any such thing—but there is One who loves you most that does know the way for you. One who knows the answers to your questions, One who knows the hard things you have been through and wants to help you.

Questions for the Almighty

Me: Father God, what do I worry about?

God: (let Him answer)

Me: Father God, what do you want me to do with my worries?

God: (pause to hear what He says & write it down)

When asking God, please know He will never contradict His Word, the Bible. He will also be encouraging and loving, because that's His character according to the Bible. Even if He is telling you something that may be hard for you to hear, like a good Father might, He will still be kind, because that is His character. Any mean voice you hear could either be yourself or the enemy of your soul.

Now, turn that worry into a prayer! (And remember, trust is a choice we get to make in every situation. It's not always a feeling.)

Prayer Pause

So let's pause to pray, because the Bible says, be anxious for nothing, but in everything by prayer and supplication with thanksgiving let your requests be made known to God. And the peace of God, which surpasses all comprehension, will guard your hearts and your minds in Christ Jesus. (See Philippians 4:6-7)

Pray this prayer or a prayer of your own heart's cry to the Lord for understanding, repentance, or help. He will answer.

Father God,

I am so grateful that You are real, that You are big, that You are powerful, and that You truly love me—whether I feel it or not. You are love, and I choose to believe it. I believe You knit me together in my mother's womb, whether anyone knew I was coming or not.

I believe You know the end from the beginning. I believe You sent Your Son to die for the anxious thoughts in my head and the healing of my mind. Thank You, Jesus, for Your peace, for Your blood, and Your forgiveness. Thank You that I can be free from worry, no matter what anyone else says.

I know and choose to believe that You are bigger than my thoughts, my feelings, what my doctors say or the world around me. You are God and I proclaim this to be true. Thank You for Your healing love. Continue to heal me and help me to arrest every thought in my head that leads me to worry.

In Jesus' mighty name, I pray!

•　•　•

*There is more hope for you
than you see right now!*

3

The Lie of
Discouragement

*You are such a loser, Lindsay. You just sit here and do
nothing.*

Something kept telling me I wasn't going to be
okay, that I was never going to leave my couch,
that God didn't care, and that I better get it
together.

The problem was, I had no idea what to get
together. I was paralyzed by discouragement and
had no idea what was wrong. Until a friend called.

"Lindsay, what's up?" he asked.

Trying to put on my happiest voice, I chatted away to him. But within a few minutes, he stopped me and said, "Lindsay, are you dealing with discouragement?"

To my own surprise, I burst into tears.

I was kind of shocked that I was crying, but then I realized he must have hit the nail on the head.

"I could tell on Sunday," he said.

I thought, *that was five days ago. How could I have been dealing with discouragement and not have even realized it? I thought I was acting really happy on Sunday. I thought I was happy on Sunday.*

I wasn't "feeling" sad, but I guess, deep down, I was. I was discouraged and hadn't even realized it.

"Self-pity is the doorway to discouragement," my friend said. "And discouragement leads to sadness and sorrow—and left unchecked can take us right into depression."

That was a lot of information for an afternoon phone call. But you know what? He was right.

Self-pity.

It was an old lie poking up to see if I might agree with it again: *Poor, poor me, no one understands.*

The truth is, someone does understand. His name is Jesus and He is Love. The enemy would love for us to feel sorry for ourselves, trust me I did for years. It got me nowhere.

We are instead powerful sons and daughters of The King and we get to make powerful decisions in our thought process. We can stand and believe the God who literally spoke the universe into existence—or not.

We choose what we believe.

I know it sounds direct, but someone had to speak this over my life and it changed everything.

See, we get to speak life or death over ourselves. Our words and thoughts have power. We must watch what comes out of our mouths.

Discouragement We Are Done Here

Discouragement loves to help us sit around and feel sorry for ourselves but that leads to more discouragement.

Hope does not disappoint, no matter how we feel.

We must do as the Bible instructs, because our Daddy wrote it. We must take every thought captive (see 2 Corinthians 10:5). Self-pity will never help us, even if it feels justified in the moment.

The truth is: hope deferred makes the heart sick, (see Proverbs 13:12). So let's hope, hope, hope and hang tightly onto hope no matter what! Let's hope in our God working things out better than we expected. Let's hope in Love Himself instead of a certain thing turning out the way we want it to.

Instead of listening to discouragement and sinking further into the couch, we must get up and tell discouragement exactly what Heaven says about hope.

Jump up and down and scream if you need to. Make your body believe it. It's not always easy, but it is simple. Hope does not disappoint. Hope is a person and we can hope in what He says. We can hope in His promises:

- He says that no weapon formed against you will prosper. (See Isaiah 54:17.)

- He says that He will work all things together for our good and His glory. (See Romans 8:28.)

- He says that we will see the goodness of the Lord in the land of the living. (See Psalm 27:13.)

We must learn to encourage ourselves. That's *en*courage, which is the opposite of *dis*courage.

"This hope we have as an anchor of the soul, a hope both sure and steadfast and one which enters within the veil…" (Hebrews 6:19)

We must speak hope to ourselves as crazy as it sounds, we must say, "No, I won't always be sitting here on my couch, confused, feeling a bit lost in life, wondering if I'll ever be okay. I know I will be okay."

And then it is absolutely beautiful to ask Papa God to help you believe what you just said in faith.

Because He is pleased with your faith.

We often have to join Him in the co-laboring and speak what is true. "No, thoughts in my head, I won't listen to your lies. I will instead choose hope, I will choose to believe hope, I will speak hope over myself no matter what you are trying to tell me."

Sometimes you've just got to get all sassy with those mean thoughts in your head.

And that's perfectly okay.

I then like to back up my thoughts with Scripture.

"We exult in hope of the glory of God. And not only this, but we also exult in our tribulations knowing that tribulation brings about perseverance and perseverance, proven character; and proven character hope and hope does not disappoint, because the love of God has been poured out within our hearts through the Holy Spirit who was given to us." (Romans 5:2b-5)

How kind is God to pour out His love into our hearts? And if you are struggling, I say ask Holy Spirit to do it again.

Say, Holy Spirit, I need more of God's love poured out into my heart right now and watch what He does.

Journal Moment

Do you struggle with self-pity or feeling sorry for yourself? Ask the Lord what to do.

Me: Lord, I need help. I need help out of self pity, what should I do?

God: (pause and let Him speak)

Remember, His answers will always line up with Scripture; they will never lead you in a different direction than His Word.

●　　●　　●

The reality He has for you is
better than you can imagine!

4

The Lie of Fantasy

I thought wondering about the future was normal. I thought it was how our brain operated. I never saw it as harmful and I don't think it is always harmful, but I have found that it can be harmful.

Let me explain.

I thought everyone wondered about the future—hopes, dreams, plans. I mean, the world celebrates planning, right? It's a must. Isn't it?

"Trust in the Lord with all your heart and do not lean on your own understanding. In all your

ways acknowledge Him, and He will make your paths straight." (Proverbs 3:5-6)

I could quote it with authority. I would tell everyone I loved this verse. I had it on my wall, on the dashboard of my car, and on my Facebook page. I even had it proudly embroidered on my tote bag. (I lived in the South for eight years. We like to carry around embroidered tote bags.)

But did I really trust God?

Did I rely on Him daily, step by step, moment by moment? Or did I worry, meditate, dwell on and fantasize about the future, really wanting control?

It's a good question to ask ourselves.

Dreaming can be powerful and I believe dreaming with God is without question Biblical. But I would suggest it can also be a stumbling block. Especially when we miss the blessing of the day we are in because we are off in La-La Land making up stories in our heads about the good or the bad of the future.

In my season of wonderment—which still tries to pop up every once in a while—I would think about my future husband. (*Was it him? Or maybe him? Oh dear, I hope not* him!)

44

It wasn't just a thought; it was an unhealthy use of my imagination. It was a lie telling me "when I get married, everything will be better."

Instead of living my current season, instead of enjoying the day I was in, I would sit and think about the future, letting those thoughts—the what ifs, the I wonder whens, the maybes—go round and round in my head. I was completely distracted from what God was showing me in the moment.

It's a pesky, but common lie that loves to steal our peace by saying: "When _____ finally happens, then I will be fulfilled. Then I will be at peace."

And that is the actual lie that steals our peace. And Peace is our inheritance, it's what we are born to live in. Plus, it's who Jesus is—and He lives inside of us. It's ours.

Peace is a fruit of His Spirit that took residence in us. It's ours and we have direct access to it.

Peace doesn't ignore reality; for instance, I don't want to be single forever and that is healthy to admit. I am forty years old as I write this book; most of my friends have children graduating high school by now. I often think about "how far behind" I am—and then that still, small whisper reminds me, "Lindsay, don't compare, that will never help you. Be thankful for your life. You have a lot to be thankful for."

He's right. Of course He is, He's God. And I am not.

I understand not getting what you want when you want it. It's frustrating. But there's a difference between being frustrated and believing the lie that says, "When I get_____ (fill in the blank), then I will be_____ (fill in blank)." Like most of you, I want what I want when I want it—but we must call a lie a lie.

There is so much wisdom in being thankful for where we are right now, how far we have come and truly trust that our God knows the desires of our hearts as we walk with Him moment by moment, enjoying Him most of all.

Journal Moment

Let's ask God if there is a lie you are believing in this area? Answer this question.

"When I get _____, then will I be _____?"

For example, "When I get <u>married</u> then I will be <u>content</u>." There is no condemnation, it's not about being perfect. But it is about renewing our minds.

I love the Graham Cooke quote that says "Enjoy the learning in every situation." This helped me so much.

As I looked at life (and dating) as a learning opportunity, it helped me enjoy each season. Because learning means growing and growing is a good thing.

Plus, I started to see that my single life could be very fun if I would just stop daydreaming it away.

When I decided (and I had to decide) to do what only a single person could do and be thankful for it, I found myself being thankful for it.

I remember when I started to travel alone and thought to myself, once I am married I will probably never have this opportunity again. It was a unique experience that was filled with adventure and excitement.

It was just me and my Heavenly Father, who loves me most. It was like a Daddy/Daughter vacation. Hanging out with Him was like hanging out with pure love.

Dreaming with the Father can be beautiful. He is Love and learning love from Him will be the most solid foundation for every dream we could ever dream.

Prayer Pause

Father God,

Thank You for the season I am in. Please help me to keep today as my focus. Help me not to "dream" my current blessings away, wishing and hoping for a season ahead.

Thank You, Jesus, that You are ultimately in control of my life and I get to enjoy it, because it is a gift from You. And for that, I am very thankful.

•　　•　　•

There is joy for
your mourning!

5

The Lie of Pain

At a Celebrate Recovery class, which is a Christ-centered, 12-Step recovery program for anyone struggling with hurt, pain or addiction of any kind, I heard someone say, "The avoidance of *feeling* pain is what leads to all compulsive behavior."

I knew that was right.

Who wants to feel pain? No one! But in John 16:33 it is recorded that we will all experience trials and tribulations.

They will come in various packages for all of us, but the truth is pain seems unavoidable in this broken world. So we must learn to process it.

If we don't choose to engage in the grieving process (even in the smallest losses of life) and give that pain over to Jesus, we will be avoiding pain. And we will eventually find an unhealthy way to cope.

For me, an unhealthy way to cope with my fear of rejection, abandonment, abuse from men was by masking it. I would pretend the pain wasn't there by numbing it with vodka after vodka after vodka.

I became so cautious around men that I couldn't function. The fear that led my life in this area was crippling.

I feared rejection so much that for decades, I believed it was my protector. I was obviously very deceived. But Fear pretended to be my friend; it said it would protect me.

In reality, Fear sealed me in a straight jacket in the area of romantic love.

Insecurity and Unworthiness acted as my bouncers when I would walk past Fear in an attempt to be myself and talk to a man. They would shove my head into shame and force my face into the fear of possible rejection. And that paralyzed me so much that I was unable to muster even a tenth of my real personality.

Sound familiar?

I was so trapped and confused I couldn't see what was going on. All I knew is that I couldn't talk to men without feeling extremely weird.

I didn't think there was a way out. I thought *weird* was just who I was. I had no idea it was a deep lie I believed for decades.

Could a lie we believe really make us feel like something is deeply wrong?

Yes. It can and it will.

But the Bible says, *"for the kingdom of God is not eating and drinking, but righteousness, peace and joy in the Holy Spirit"* (Romans 14:17). So the areas of our life that aren't marked by the characteristics of the Kingdom still lie in the shadows of false beliefs.

As I would attempt to talk with a man, shame would slam my face against the wall and tell me, "He would never like you. You're an idiot."

The internal fight inside our souls is hard because no one else can tell what's going on—except for Father God.

The fear that was lying to me, pretending to protect me, was actually doing the exact opposite. It was telling me I would die if I ever got hurt again by a man. Literally. I thought I would *die*.

I remember talking to my friend as she told me a story about a relationship she'd been in with a guy she really liked for many years, and how it ended. My blood pressure shot up. I felt her pain. I blurted out, "Didn't you feel like you were going to die?"

She stared at me, surprised by the depth of my dark thought, as I started to cry. I was scared for her, scared of the pain she must have felt. When I told her how the pain of rejection from a man truly made me feel like I was going to die, she kindly said, "Lindsay, that is not normal. Let's ask God about that."

The truth is everything looks normal to you, if you don't know it's not.

Believing that I would die if a guy I thought was cute didn't like me isn't normal or healthy—but I lived that way.

For 39 years.

As Fear was pretending to keep me safe, it was also causing me to want control. I feared all the pain of my past experiences.

So I attempted to control my circumstances, and the pain would stay hidden. And as much as I thought that would help me, it was sabotaging every area of dating in my life.

It was allowing the lie to string me along like a puppet, causing me to resist the thing God knew would bring me freedom—a simple but not easy trust in the One who loved me most, Jesus Christ.

We have all been hurt by people, but Scripture is very clear that our real fight is not against people, but against powers, against the rulers of the darkness of this world, against spiritual wickedness in high places. (See Ephesians 6:12). And we have authority over all of this, because we are hidden with Christ in God.

Pain that we don't give to God will keep us in our suffering. And that is just what the devil would like—to cause pain and keep us stuck in it.

He lies to us when we are very young and it begins to entangle us. I am telling you this to expose it, because once the darkness is exposed, it loses its power.

Process The Pain

We must release the pain. We must let it out, even if it takes screaming in the car before we walk into the house. We must cry and let anger out of our body, then we must forgive those around us and hand our pain over to Jesus.

This can happen multiple times in life or multiple times about a particular situation. There are no rules and no formula to freedom; it's about being with Jesus and asking Him to help you, because He will. He will show you the way out of your pain. He will show you how to process that which needs to be processed and to forgive those who need to be forgiven.

The freedom that will open up in front of you will be miraculous.

Only God knows what you need. Ask Him to reveal it to you. He will.

Let's ask Him now!

Journal Moment

Me: Father God, how are you praying for me in this pain that has come to mind as I read this book?

God: (pause and let Him answer)

Someone once told me in a devastating time of life not to get stuck in the pain, but to go through to the beautiful part. I hated hearing that in my place of suffering—but it gave me a hope, a little hope that there *was* a beautiful part.

I would find myself screaming in my car, so mad about things that happened in my past, ways I had been hurt that weren't in God's plan for my life. But because the world is broken, we all get hurt. I would scream and cry in my car, alone, just to get to a place where I could forgive the ones who hurt me and hand my pain over to Jesus. I literally handed it to Him as if He was sitting right there consoling me, waiting to take this pain away so I could step forward once again.

Crying is like throwing up. It's gross and kind of hurts coming out—but once it's out, you feel so much better.

The Heart

We all struggle with things and that's okay.

As I continued to fiercely protect my heart in an unhealthy way without really knowing it, I got to a place where the Lord was peeling back layer after layer after layer through various circumstances. And it was hard.

I asked Him one day to show me what my heart looked like.

Suddenly I saw a picture in my minds eye of a shriveled-up grape.

Shocked, I asked, "Lord why does my heart look like a shriveled-up grape?" He immediately replied, "It's tired, Lindsay; it's worn out from overprotecting itself."

Wrecked, I knew it was God. It made so much sense. I knew without a doubt this was true. And I knew He was showing me the true state of my heart so He could restore it.

In that moment, I knew this was exactly what I had been doing all my life: protecting myself for fear of getting hurt beyond repair.

It was sad to realize all the energy I'd wasted,. But at the same time I was relieved to know the cause of so much of my struggle. God always reveals with the intention to heal.

We must trust God with all of our hearts.

I wasn't trusting God with *any* of my heart. But since God really does know what's best for His created ones, He knew my heart needed His help. He knew this habit of overprotecting myself wasn't helping me. I struggled because I was going against what He said would be best.

The Bible says we can ask God for wisdom and He will give it to us without measure (See James 1:5).

I love asking the Creator of the universe for wisdom. I mean, He has *all* the wisdom.

It's like an open book test, how nice is God?

As we walk with God through life, (the amazing and the painful), I have come to realize that I am okay after the pain has been felt and released. After I allow myself to feel the emotion and give it to Jesus, I can step forward.

But if we avoid feeling the emotion, stuffing it down because we think it is too hard to handle, it won't help us.

I love how God leads us. He is so gentle to peel back the layers that He knows needs His healing touch.

I know it can sound overwhelming. *Where do I start?* Well, as it says in James 1:5, you can ask Him for wisdom and He will give it without measure. Therefore, you can ask Him where to start.

He Created You and Loves You Most

He is so personal and loving and will lead you in the way He knows you need to go. That is part of trusting Him.

He is the healer. He will bring the right people into your life to help you. He will lead you to the right Scripture and book of the Bible. He is our first go-to and then He will lead from there, if we will allow Him.

If it feels like too much to handle, be still and know He is God. (See Psalm 46:10.) He will do the healing. Don't stop asking or inviting Him in; He knows it all anyway. Go to Him with your pain. He can take your pain and your anger. And He can give you peace and joy in place of it. It might take time, but with Him all things are possible.

Your healing is possible.

Your healing is His desire.

The thing that helps us through is Jesus, and prayer, and community. Jesus does weep with us, and comforts us if we will allow Him. *"Weeping may last for the night, but a shout of joy comes in the morning"* (Psalm 30:5). Often I have found myself in deep tears one evening, and then feeling cleansed by my crying the next day.

> *"Now faith is the assurance of things hoped for, the conviction of things not seen"* (Hebrews 11:1).

My encouragement for you is that you hope. Hope against everything you feel that says there is no hope. Grieve when you need to, yes, but hope even more!

I have felt hopelessness creeping in many times in my life. But I have learned to profess hope in the face of my pain. I have learned that sitting in my pain and feeling sorry for myself doesn't help me.

It's not one or the other; it's both. Feel the pain and then hope!

You can't actually hope too much; you must hope when it hurts most. Declare to the heavens that your Hope is in Christ. And you will see the goodness of the Lord in the land of the living (paraphrase of Psalm 27:13).

Not all things that happen to us are good, not even close, but He is a redeemer and restorer and He can cause all things to work together for our good. That is His promise, not mine. Let's hold onto it.

Our God will not only help us, He will strengthen us and uphold us in His righteous right hand! (See Isaiah 41:10.)

Journal Moment

I write to process my feelings. How do you process yours?

Let's ask Him now:

Me: Father, is there any pain that I need to process?

God: (let Him show you)

Then ask Him, *Father will you show me how?*

God: (let Him show you)

Be encouraged He will!

Prayer Pause

Father God,

The pain is too much for me to bear alone. I need Your peace in this moment. I need Your love. Please come fill me with Your peace and love as I am here to receive from Your Holy Spirit. I surrender the fact that I can't do it alone; only You can help me through. So come now and fill me to overflowing with Your power made perfect in my weakness.

In Jesus' mighty name, I pray.

•   •   •

You are worthy of freedom!

6

The Lie of Unforgiveness

Like me, you may have heard the old adage, "Unforgiveness is like drinking poison and expecting the other person to die." But in reality, you are only killing yourself.

I held deep unforgiveness in my heart toward myself, other people and even God. The problem was I went through life without knowing that was my problem.

I knew something wasn't right.

I knew I had been hurt a lot in life and done a lot of things to hurt myself. But I didn't know how much my inability to forgive was destroying me.

Unfortunately, no one will get through this life without having to forgive someone for *some*thing. That's why Jesus told His disciples we are to forgive seventy times seven—which is 490 times, even if it is the same person. Even if it's 490 times a *day*—or more.

Sounds a little harsh, but Jesus knew that unforgiveness would ultimately take us down if it wasn't dealt with properly.

The Soul

The pain lodged in my soul was deep and destructive and needed to be released.

The only way to true freedom is to choose to forgive.

I wanted freedom. So with list in hand of all the people who had hurt me, I realized quickly the two hardest people to forgive were myself and God.

God doesn't need my forgiveness, but I needed to forgive Him. For my own sake.

From my perspective, God allowed the pain in my life, and that made me really really mad. It didn't seem fair. It didn't seem to be what everyone else went through, so why me?

We can all ask, "Why me?" God isn't afraid of our questions. But comparison and the victim mentality will only lead us right into a black hole.

What we must remember is that people are broken. We are broken. And the world we live in is broken.

In a broken world, we will make mistakes. Sometimes we will be careless and there will be areas in which we are weak. Since the dictionary defines unforgiveness as not allowing for mistakes, carelessness, or weakness, we see how this cycle can go if we don't learn to forgive.

We all need forgiveness *from* others, and we all need forgiveness *for* others.

Forgiveness is the foundation of our faith, for *all have sinned and fall short of the glory of God* (Romans 3:23), but God sent His Only Son, Jesus, to be a sacrifice for our sins, so we could be forgiven. And because of this, God expects those who have been forgiven to forgive.

My forgiveness journey didn't happen all at once. It happened in stages led by the Holy Spirit. His grace gave me the ability to supernaturally forgive at some points. And then God Himself led me to books, workshops, visions, and to the altar at church to help me release forgiveness at other points. If we ask for His help, He will lead us to the path of freedom, because He is freedom.

We can be encouraged, because Jesus came to set us free. That means He will do the work in and through us. We must trust and believe and take the steps He leads us to take.

We must believe He will help us, and going to Him directly for help is the wisest thing we can do in life. He is so ready to help us with anything we need.

The Process of Forgiveness

Forgiveness may happen in a variety of ways. I remember times when He would bring a thought to my mind while I was sitting in the middle of traffic or standing at the sink washing dishes. He was asking me to forgive a certain person in a certain situation.

It isn't always the big things in life. It can be the smaller things that bring offense. It happens because we are human, but we must be aware of what is going on in our hearts to protect them. Not in an overprotective way (like shriveled-up grape hearts), but in a way that keeps them clean of offense, unforgiveness, and bitterness.

Torment

Spiritually speaking, the Bible talks about unforgiveness being reason enough to be turned over to the tormentors. Stay with me here, in Matthew 18, Jesus tells us a parable in which a master forgave his slave a large sum of money (that's like God forgiving us).

But then that slave had a debt owed to him and he refused to forgive his slave (that's like us not forgiving others). The master was so angry that Scripture says that he handed him over to the jailers to be tortured, until he should pay back all he owed. (See Matthew 18:34.)

In other versions of the Bible the language: "tormentors" is used.

I know we don't like these passages, but there they are. And from my personal experience, this is very true.

I would suggest that Jesus knows just how important forgiveness is. So in His kindness He allows us to be tormented into forgiving others. You don't have to agree with me, but this is how I see it.

We have all sinned and fallen short of the glory of God. He forgives us the debts we could never pay back. But then we hold things against other humans and won't forgive them like our Father in Heaven forgave us. And God is not okay with our double standard.

As soon as I started to forgive people who had hurt me, a lot of my nagging medical issues went away.

Please hear me.

I'm not saying that everyone who is sick has unforgiveness in their lives. I can't say that and, frankly, I *wouldn't* say that. I know I still have a lot of medical issues—and I feel as though I have forgiven just about everyone, including myself, God and others.

But even non-spiritual research says forgiving people comes with health benefits. And when medicine and the Bible line up, I get excited.

So, let's forgive.

1. Say this out loud: "I choose to forgive _____ from my heart for _____ (what he/she did to me)."

2. Next, say out loud: "I cancel all debts or obligations owed to me by _____ for what they did to me."

3. Say out loud: "I forgive myself for any pain I caused myself with this memory and the unforgiveness I have been carrying."

Journal Moment

It's not always the big ugly things of our past that need our attention in the forgiveness department. And that is why it is important to ask God "who is it, Lord, that I need to forgive?" He will be faithful to show you. Ask Him now.

Me: Father, please bring to mind who I need to forgive?

God: (*listen and see who comes to mind*)

You may need to make a list and come back to it later. I get that. I did that more than once. It's okay. It's healthy. It's healing to your soul. It honors God and opens up the door to freedom.

List for later:

1.
2.

3.

4.

5.

6.

7.

8

9.

10.

If you don't feel different after you forgive, that's okay. Forgiveness is not a feeling. It's an act of your will.

It's about making a choice in obedience to God—because He knows unforgiveness hurts you.

When we wrestle with God on this (I just call it like I see it), we throw "adult temper tantrums." That's because basically we're saying, "I don't want to, God. I don't want to forgive them."

We want to hold onto the anger because it feels justified—and to be honest, it feels good. It feels like we are getting back at the person who hurt us by staying angry. But the truth says:

"For our struggle is not against flesh and blood, but against the rulers, against the powers, against the world forces of this darkness, against the

spiritual forces of wickedness in the heavenly places" (Ephesians 6:12).

The people we sometimes refuse to forgive are not our problem. But the enemy would love for us to think they are. That's because he is really the problem.

So what do we do? The very next verse in the Bible says:

"Therefore, take up the full armor of God, so that you will be able to resist in the evil day, and having done everything, to stand firm. Stand firm therefore, having girded your lions with truth, and having put on the breastplate of righteousness, and having shod your feet with the preparation of the gospel of peace" (Ephesians 6:13-15).

The very next verse says:

"in addition to all, taking up the shield of faith with which you will be able to extinguish all the flaming arrows of the evil one. And take the helmet of salvation, and the sword of the Spirit, which is the word of God" (Ephesians 6:13-15).

When I saw that the Scripture read, *you can extinguish all the flaming arrows of the evil one with this shield of faith* (See Ephesians 6:16), I got excited. The word *all* is a big promise.

I will admit I have really struggled in the past with believing the lie that the devil is more powerful than God. And let me tell you, believing *that* will create gripping fear in your life for decades, if not a lifetime.

We must remember we have a big God and a little devil. And we have been given all power and authority through Jesus Christ.

Prayer Pause

Father God,

Thank You for Jesus, thank You for Holy Spirit. Thank You that I am never alone; thank You that even when I don't feel Your embrace, Your Word says You will never leave me or forsake me. Fill me with Your love, with You, because You are love. I need more of You, Lord.

In Jesus' Name, I pray.

•   •   •

7

The Lie of Control

As I sat at our church retreat listening to a message on idolatry, I wondered, "What are my idols?"

We all have those things that can slip up and take their place ahead of God in our hearts. And because they are often disguised as "good things," we don't always notice right away that they've become idols. Thankfully, if we ask Jesus, He will kindly show us.

I started to pray, trying to figure out what my idols were.

"Is it sugar?"

"Is it coffee?"

I headed to the front of the auditorium to pray. That is where you can usually find me, praying on my knees, not sure what to do.

As I prayed for understanding of my anxious heart, I kept hearing this phrase over and over again in my mind:

Trying to figure it out.
Trying to figure it out.
Trying to figure it out.

All of the sudden it hit me. My idol was my obsession with "trying to figure it out."

Figure out what? I wondered.

"Everything, Lindsay," God said. "You are trying to figure out everything, including your idols."

He was right. And like a good father, He and I had a good giggle. I mean that is kind of funny.

I realized I wanted control because I still feared I couldn't really trust God with my heart or my life.

I trust Him in a lot of areas—but He wants it all. He knows He is the safest place for us. He is such a good dad, but it takes us so long to realize it sometimes. Especially if life has been hard, it feels like it's His fault.

But the world is broken

And He doesn't cause the pain.

Our God is so much more fun than we give Him credit for. He created joy, and as much pain as we endure in life, there is so much more joy to be had as well.

He weeps with us. But He also finds joy in us and our funny ways and loves to bring joy into our lives.

Questioning God

What I have learned about God is that He is not scared of our questions. In fact, He welcomes them.

In that moment at the altar, He was answering my question about my idols. He was freeing me from myself.

I would constantly torment myself with questions like:

What is the next step in my career?
Who is my future husband?
Who are the false prophets?
When is the world going to end?
What is my calling in life?
How is God going to save all the people I love?

These were obsessions, idols in my life. I put these questions above God—running scenarios through my head, desperately trying to figure out what might happen in this situation or that one.

I was basically worrying about the future. And we've already learned that worry is really torment.

But Scripture says:

"Trust in the LORD with all your heart and do not lean on your own understanding. In all your ways acknowledge Him, and he will make your paths straight" (Proverbs 3:5–6).

Trusting God does not mean trying to figure things out. Rather it is praying, asking for His wisdom moment by moment, surrendering to His ways each step. It's trusting that He knows the end from the beginning and that He will not leave us or forsake us.

Even in Dating

I don't know about you, but whenever I try to surrender and trust in the One who created me with things that I really wonder about—like who I should marry or even just date, or when a guy is going to ask me on a date, or *will* a guy ever ask me on a date?—I hear a nagging voice inside my head say, "Just pick a guy, Lindsay. It can't be that hard, everyone else in the world does it. You are so dumb. You are getting old."

That is the lie.

The liar of our souls would love to trick us into making a decision out of desperation rather than from being led by God.

I believe God gives us a choice in our spouses. After all, if He doesn't make us choose Him, why on earth would He make us choose a certain person? But I do believe that we can be in such a place of desperation that we choose out of fear because we believe what we really want isn't possible.

There was a point in my life when I would date guys I didn't find attractive because in my twisted mindset, I thought if I dated a guy who thought I was the most attractive girl he could get, he wouldn't leave me for another woman.

That is called controlling out of the fear of abandonment. Thankfully, the Lord in His kind wisdom showed me I did this. And even though I am still single, the things I have learned since then have transformed my understanding of my worth and what I am looking for in a husband. But it took time—and if we are so worried about timing, we could very well make a bad decision out of brokenness.

We can do these things in our own strength. Or we can choose to trust our perfect Heavenly Father who wants us to walk in His Spirit, with His Son, asking Him for wisdom step by step. He will help us. I know because He has helped me.

Journal Moment

It's a good process to ask your Heavenly Father, who loves you most, what your idols might be.

Let's ask Him now.

Me: Father, what are my idols?

God:

Me: How can I surrender them to You?

God:

•　　•　　•

8

The Lie of Unworthiness

Was it that simple?

After all these years?

I wanted to stand up on the airplane and yell, "The Devil is a liar!" when the reality popped into my head. I was headed to Colorado for a retreat, and as I walked down the aisle of the airplane to my seat, I sensed the Lord was answering a question I had been asking for a long time.

Struggling to feel safe in any kind of romantic relationship, I had been asking the Lord why. I wondered what was wrong with me. I had tried and tried to figure it out. But it wasn't until I asked God, "How long am I going to have to wait to get over my fear of marriage?" that He responded, "Until you walk through it." Which wasn't really what I wanted to hear.

A few months later, I felt the Lord asking me a question. "Lindsay," He said, "do you really want to get married? Because you don't have to."

After deep reflection, some face-on-the-floor prayer time and facing a ton of tears, I said something that was hard for me to say. "Yes, Lord, I do. Even though I know it's not all rainbows and puppy dogs, the answer is still yes—I do desire marriage."

It was hard to push past the fear that gripped my life for decades in that area—the potential pain of rejection and abandonment, the lies that screamed at me constantly, saying I would not be okay if I were rejected or abandoned, which simply isn't true.

God heals all pain, if we allow Him—even our greatest fear.

I felt completely unworthy of the kind of man I desired. I felt I was unlovable because of all my flaws. My self-hatred was hidden deep and destroying dreams in my heart that I didn't even know I had.

I spent a decade of my life in such fear and insecurity that I depended on alcohol to even *fake* self-confidence when it came to men. I believed such hateful things about myself that I didn't want to live anymore. But no one knew. You couldn't see it on the outside, but it was eating my soul alive on the inside.

Fear will do that and self hatred will assist.

Once I came to know the Lord, He began what was a longer than expected healing process— one I never would have chosen to go through, but know was necessary in my life to move forward and out of this lie of fear.

But the question still remained: what was holding me back?

I was "that girl"—the one who would often say, "I trust Jesus so much that I believe He can bring my husband to my front door. I mean, He created the universe."

That was, until that moment on the beach when I asked God how long I would have to wait to overcome my fear of marriage and He said, "Until you walk through it."

He then said I was unknowingly using my strong faith to hide and protect myself, and that I needed to step out of the boat and trust Him in this area.

I have passed up many opportunities in my life to enter into a romantic relationship, all out of fear.

I have walked through many of my fears. I thought I had overcome this one too—until I was faced with it again.

I suddenly realized how weird I was in front of men.

Still.

If they were cute (in my eyes), I was weird. If I didn't find them attractive, I was weird. It was all very weird.

I needed and wanted to get to the bottom of this "weird."

So, I prayed. I cried and I asked the One who created me to dig it out even if it hurts.

Six months later, He answered. I found myself on a sabbatical from work, which had way more to do with getting to the bottom of some of my wrong thinking in regards to men and marriage than anything else.

It seems He took me up on the "even if it hurts" part. I often found myself lying on the kitchen floor weeping through my fears, crying so hard I was almost unable to catch my breath.

He was bringing up the pain that caused me to believe the lies about marriage and men so I could overcome them. He had indeed answered my prayer.

Back to the Plane

As I sat on that airplane—my sanctuary in the sky—on my way to Colorado, I realized I felt completely unworthy of a good marriage, or a husband I was genuinely attracted to.

All of a sudden I thought, "Wait. What?"

Could this whole mess be good, old-fashioned unworthiness?

Twenty-plus years of self-sabotage due to fear was caused by a sense of unworthiness?

Could it be true?

I was ticked, livid at the ability a lie had to hold me back in such a fierce way.

Sometimes the enemy wants to complicate things. He wants to steal our identity and take with it our entire destiny.

But he can't control us. All he can do is deceive us. And I was deceived for a long time about who I was and what I was created for.

When I looked up the word "worthy" in the dictionary, it said, being good enough to be considered important. I didn't think I had good enough qualities to be considered a wife of a man I was attracted to.

How dare the devil, the father of lies, lie to me all these years and tell me I wasn't worthy of love!

He lied to me and told me I wasn't good enough, that no man would ever really like me, that marriage would destroy me, that I would be unable to love my husband. How dare he lie to me!

This revelation in my life came in layers. God used everything in my life to peel back one layer at a time. It was a process I had to walk through, just like He promised.

It was painful at times, I won't lie. But it was worth every single moment and every single tear.

Freedom

I have never felt so free, so sure of myself, so sure of my true identity, with so many lies I used to believe about myself gone.

Am I perfect? Hardly. But am I healthy? Absolutely.

Jesus won this one.

Jesus wins all of them.

Much of my wrong thinking has been replaced with His truth, which has birthed a new sense of hope and joy in my life.

The walking-out process toward marriage is still moment by moment for me. But I believe everything in life should be walked out step by step with our Creator, Savior and King. We will never *not* need Him. He designed us that way.

I realized while writing this book that my biggest fear, my biggest desire and my biggest dream were all to get married. My biggest dream was stuffed under my biggest fear. He reveals it all in such layers and all for our good.

Journal Moment

Me: Father, what are my biggest fears?

God: (*let Him whisper to you*)

Me: Father, what is my deepest desire?

God: (*let Him reply*)

Me: Father, what is my greatest dream?

God: (*let Him help you if you don't know*)

We are His, and He is ours. He will lead us, if we allow Him. He is still leading me toward marriage, but my eyes are now fixed on Him. He leads me through all the stepping-out-of-the-boat moments and jumping-back-in-because-*that*-didn't-work-out-so-well moments.

He shows me the win in the situation, the growth. *My* growth.

For example, after a few of my "out of the boat" risks that didn't work out so well, I felt stupid for thinking "Guy 718 would ever like me." (I use Guy 718 not because there have been that many guys in my life, but rather to protect the innocent.)

It was that same old lie. I believed it again. But I could see how God was working, because I knew a lot sooner that this "feeling stupid" thing wasn't from God.

Plus, let's be honest. My awkward factor had dramatically decreased this time. That's a win. I saw God was working. That alone helped me have hope that He was on the case and leading me toward something good. Something really, really good.

And then that time when God asked me to forgive the entire male population

At one point, God showed me that I had unforgiveness toward the entire male gender. Yep, that was problematic. He showed me how I had more grace for women than I did for men, and that I needed to forgive the entire male population.

When He said this, I laughed out loud, because it sounded so absurd. But you know those times when someone says something and they are serious and you think it's a joke, so you laugh and they don't? It was like that: I laughed and He didn't. It was like a good father, telling you what you need to do. You think He's being ridiculous, but then you look at Him and see how serious He really is.

That was us.

So I did it. It was simple, no real emotion connected to it. Nothing felt different, no lighting bolts from Heaven, just simple obedience that I know opened up a huge place in my heart.

Journal Moment

How about you? Is God working on you in some area? Ask Him. He is faithful to reveal and give wisdom (see James 1:5). Let's ask Him.

Me: Father God, is there something you want to show me?

God:

Me: Is there something I am scared of?

God:

Me: Is there something I feel unworthy of?

Ask God if there is anything holding you back from whatever you know you desire, but feel far from. He may just have something to reveal to you—always for your good and His glory.

Me: Father, is there something holding me back from what I desire?

God:

Me: Father is there something I feel unworthy of that You want me to know I am worthy of?

God:

And remember, just take one step at a time. It's why He says, "Walk with Me." We hold His hand and walk with Him step by step. We keep our eyes on Jesus.

God is our Creator. Everything was created by Him. He is the final authority in all things. We get to choose to believe that or not.

We are brothers and sisters of Jesus, and He is the Son of God. I don't think we always realize who we are once we become followers of Jesus; we don't often take on our new identity. We are still a bit tangled up in the old one. We become the new person once we believe, but we still struggle to believe it. The Bible says, *"For as he thinks within himself, so he is"* (Proverbs 23:7.)

Therefore, I would suggest if we believe we are unworthy, we are. I have seen this very thing manifest in my life. My beliefs became my reality. And I walked it out. But not in God's eyes; He knows who we are and He longs for us to know who we are as well.

•   •   •

*You are fully and completely
loved as you are!*

9

The Lie of Fear

Caring at all what people think is exhausting. Trying to protect or manage everyone's perceptions of you won't work. I know, I tried.

Fear is not usually isolated to just one thing; it tends to penetrate to other areas of life.

For me, it felt like I was being intensely harassed and bullied. I couldn't escape.

It felt as though I was in the prison of my very own soul. The fear I was dealing with was of the devil. I constantly wondered what he would try next and if I would ever break free. I thought he had the power to kill me—and that he was going to.

But then I learned the devil only has the power we give him. He is indeed real and can torment and harass us. But only when we buy into his lies do we give him major power in our lives.

At points in my journey, I almost thought more about the devil than I did about God. I actually believed for a long part of my Christian walk—especially after moving to Los Angeles— that the devil was more powerful than God. I can't even explain the terror and destruction that lie will cause in your life.

What Scripture confirms about the devil is that he is the father of lies (See John 8:44). We get the free will to either agree with what he is saying about us or what God is saying about us.

I believe in casting the devil out of our lives. For me, that came in layers and in different forms.

My favorite quote recently on this subject is from the evangelist Todd White, who said, "You can't fight the devil. It's like punching air. You instead have to fill your head so full of the Word of God that there is no room for the devil's lies."

When Todd said this at a conference I was attending, I literally jumped out of my seat yelling, "Yes! Yes!" I was so excited, because everything in my head was saying the opposite. I needed to hear this.

I needed to know it was true.

On the way to this particular conference, I almost got hit by a train. I found myself in the middle of the tracks with the gate down around my car! The engineer had been alerted that someone was stuck on the tracks and managed to stop before hitting me. But as you can imagine, I was shaken to the core.

I immediately thought, *the enemy just tried to kill me!* Then I heard a strong, authoritative and kind voice say, "Don't you tell anyone this, Lindsay."

I wondered why not. And then the Lord said, "Lindsay, you keep giving the enemy credit. You haven't realized that no matter what he tries, I am the One protecting you. You were getting ready to give the enemy credit for trying to run you over with a train, but you have failed to realize I am the One who protected you."

Three Kinds of Fear

A sweet friend once told me there are three kinds of fear that all other fears are rooted in.

1. Fear of man (a.k.a. people pleasing)
2. Fear of the devil
3. Fear of death

I told my friend I definitely had been struggling with the first two. The third didn't seem to be as bad for me. But later, I realized that all my fear came tumbling back to this feeling of death.

So what is the cure? How do we fight fear?

We start by going to 1 John 4:18:

"There is no fear in love; but perfect love casts out fear, because fear involves punishment, and the one who fears is not perfected in love."

It sounds painfully simple. I mean, thirty-nine years of fear and this little prayer was going to do the trick?

Simpler Than We Sometimes Believe

Another friend of mine sent me a message, super excited about a major breakthrough people were having at a prayer meeting at church. He was so pumped because there is nothing more beautiful than watching people break free from the lies that hold them captive.

He knew about all the sickness I had been experiencing over the previous month (and to be honest, most of my life). But in this particular season it was one thing after another. And each "pain" came with a truckload of fear barreling in behind it. I felt completely nuts for having a different pain every other day. It was obnoxious.

Then I started to get a little insight, that this was deeper than just a mysterious physical pain. I knew the root was spiritual, and the culprit was fear.

My friend's next message to me said, "Lindsay, do you want to take care of that fear tonight?"

Without a second thought, I said, "Of course."

I then got a series of texts from him telling me how to do that.

1. **Recognize** the fear (whatever "it" is).
2. Take **responsibility** before God for partnering with fear.
3. **Repent** to the Father in the name of Jesus.
4. **Renounce** fear in the name of Jesus.
5. **Remove** it!

6. **Resist** that fear when it tries to come back (2 Corinthians 10:5—take every thought captive and submit it to the will of Christ).

7. **Rejoice**. Now that you are free, give God thanks and praise.

8. **Restore** someone else.

In the next text, he wrote: "Ask the Father to tell you what you need to repent of specifically concerning fear. Could it be movies, men, past experiences, any place where you've partnered with fear and allowed the enemy to establish his kingdom?"

Then: "No condemnation, just responsibility and you will receive forgiveness so quickly it will blow your mind."

As I read that, as clear as day, three words came to my mind.

Foundation.

Protection.

Security.

I repented. I quietly said, "Oh Lord, forgive me for making my foundation in life fear instead of You and for seeing fear as my protector and security because the truth is that is You. I was wrong."

The Bible is so clear.

"For no man can lay a foundation other than the one which is laid, which is Jesus Christ" (1 Corinthians 3:11).

Jesus is my foundation as a believer, But I had made fear my foundation by accident.

Thankfully, the Bible says, "We can ask for wisdom from God and He will give it to us without measure" (James 1:5). Obviously my fav scripture.

My friend then said to me, "Maybe it was a guiding spirit to a false comforter," referring to fear. I knew deep within my soul that was exactly what had been going on.

I was putting fear in place of the Holy Spirit.

The Holy Spirit is our Helper. The Bible says so in John 14:26, but I had been giving fear that place in my life. Fear was the one helping me in every decision I made.

But not anymore!

I was free! I knew it. I woke up the next day with a joy I had not known before then.

Journal Moment

In Psalm 51, David cries to God in repentance for the pattern of sin he engaged in following his transgressions with Bathsheba. He offers us a picture of what repentance should look like in our lives.

1. David acknowledges his sin.
2. He asks for forgiveness.
3. He then asks God to renew him.
4. Finally, he asks God to help him teach others.

Sounds familiar, doesn't it?
Now it's your turn! Go for it!

Me: Father God, what fear do You want me to repent of?

God:

•   •   •

There is a garment
of praise for heaviness!

10

The Lie of Rejection

Rejection can seep in on the playground, at your church, in your family, or at the office, without ever being spotted. It's slimy, and it's always evil—straight from the pit of Hell.

The enemy is always the enemy. So no matter if rejection got to you through a friend, a pastor, a spouse, or a family member, it's never the people we are fighting with. It's always the enemy.

Now, does the enemy love to work through people? Absolutely, no question. That is his primary way. And if he can do it through someone super-close to you, he knows that will hurt the worst. This is why forgiving the people around you is so paramount.

As the Bible says in 1 Peter 5:8:

"Be of sober spirit, be alert. Your adversary, the devil, prowls around like a roaring lion, seeking someone to devour."

Therefore, friends, we must fight—but we don't fight alone, and we don't fight against flesh and blood (See Ephesians 6:12). Truthfully, it's not even our fight; the Lord says He will fight *for* us.

In my experience, we do play a part. It's simple, but for some reason it doesn't always *feel* simple. We must keep our eyes on Jesus Christ, for the Bible says, *"The steadfast of mind You will keep in perfect peace, because he trusts in You"* (Isaiah 26:3.)

Basically, keeping our minds on Him will give us perfect peace, because we are trusting in Him!

Easier said than done, I know, but it is true.

When we have been hurt by someone, either in our past or in our current situation, we have to forgive them. It's oddly dangerous not to forgive.

We must forgive all those who have rejected us in our past, or even seemingly rejected us. We must also be aware that self-rejection can cause a lot of our problems; this comes from self-hatred.

Self-rejection and self-hatred were at the root of so many of my problems, but I didn't know until I dug and dug and dug to the bottom.

You can go straight to the root and yank it out. You can get what took me decades in a moment.

Prayer Pause

Father God,

I received the truth of who You call me. I am a beloved daughter of the King of Glory and I here and now declare that I am accepted by You and by myself. I also declare that I am loved by You and by myself. I come out of agreement that I hate myself or that I reject myself. I want to follow You and that is not Your best for me.

I choose to be obedient and begin this journey of self love and self acceptance right now, I know You will lead me and guide me on my way. I come out of agreement with the lie that this is selfish. I want to love like You love and I must learn to love and accept myself in a healthy way in order to love and serve others.

The Good News

Focusing on your issues won't set you free. Focusing on the opposite will.

Step 1: We must renew our minds with the truth. We must practice things that are hard for us.

We must accept the fact that we are loved by the God Who created us. Even if our parents didn't know we were coming, our perfect Heavenly Father knew. And not only did He know, He planned it with a purpose for you, and is very, very excited that you are here. He is love, and He loves you most.

Love Himself created you and loves you most.

Learning to receive God's love is where we must start, after receiving forgiveness for everything we have ever even thought about doing, through the work of the blood of Jesus Christ.

After we have accepted His sacrifice for us to be redeemed and restored to perfection in the Father's eyes, the next step is to learn to receive

God's love. That is hard for almost everyone, because we don't feel worthy of such a love. But that is just what Jesus died for, so not learning to receive it will tell Jesus His pain and suffering had no purpose.

Step 2: Once we begin to learn the love our Father has for us (it's a life-long, moment-by-moment journey), we can then learn to love Him back with the love He has given to us.

Scripture tells us we only love because He loved us first. It also says the first commandment is to love the Lord God with all your heart, soul, mind and strength.

Isn't it sweet that our God gives us all we need to do what He asks us to do?

Once we begin to love the Lord God with all our heart, soul, mind and strength, we are to love our neighbor as ourselves.

What I realized in my journey as I tried so hard to love others was that I didn't love myself.

I would try and try to love others out of straight obedience to the Lord, but it wasn't with His love. It was a love based in fear, because I feared what God would do if I didn't do what He said.

So I had to take a step back. I didn't want to. I wanted to move forward. But He knew I wouldn't make it very far in my purpose for Him if I didn't learn this foundation of loving myself.

I found it so hard. I thought it sounded selfish, self-focused. I felt so much condemnation. But now I know that was from the Liar. He also knew this was the key to my destiny. He knew once I understand this, I would become unstoppable in showing the love of the Lord to everyone I met.

Loving yourself is a journey and that's okay. It is an issue with most people, particularly women. I only know this because after speaking to a pastor friend of mine who counsels countless women, he said nine times out of ten their issue is self-hatred. (I would add to that "self-rejection.")

So, ladies and gentlemen, we must ask our Father, Who knows us best and adores us most, what our next step in this journey is. I share my testimonies with you, but I will never promise you a formula. We don't need a formula; we need a Papa.

And that's God.

We need a Counselor and a Comforter who has all the time in the world to talk to us and help us through all we struggle with, and that's Holy Spirit.

We need a Best Friend who is perfectly fun and kind and loving and for us. And that is Jesus!

•   •   •

11

The Lie of Abandonment

I have struggled with each one of the following issues, so if they sound familiar to you, no worries. You are in good company!

- Do you attach too quickly to people?

- Do you exhibit excessive controlling behaviors (or thoughts)?

- Do you find flaws in potential mates before you even embark on a relationship with them?

- Do you sabotage your relationships?

- Do you have constant fears of someone cheating on you? Or fear that you will cheat on someone else?

- Do you expect perfection from yourself and other people?

- Do you have commitment issues?

If you resonate with one or more of these questions, you may need a touch from your Heavenly Father. Let Him apply His love to heal your beautiful heart.

He is so good at this.

So be encouraged.

Similar to rejection, abandonment can come from many sources at different times in life.

And knowing "it" has a name and speaking it will help us get free!

The enemy loves to tell us, "This is just who you are!" He always wants to attack our identity, which never allows us the freedom to overcome that which Jesus bought on the cross.

Not only is our inheritance freedom, as followers of Jesus, Romans 8:37 also says we are more than conquers.

The truth is, you are *not* your issues!

THE LIE: I use to think I was such a disaster there was literally no hope.

THE TRUTH: God showed me I was wrong and that there is always hope in Him!

> *"It was for freedom that Christ set us free; therefore, keep standing firm and do not be subject again to a yoke of slavery"* (Galatians 5:1).

The "feelings of abandonment" can seep into our thoughts about the future and tell us that what happened in the past is going to happen in the future. Then fear manifests on top of abandonment.

These are both lies.

The Bible calls lies "yokes of slavery." It is literally telling us not to be subject to (in some translations it says "do not let yourselves be burdened again") by a yoke of slavery.

There is a part for us to play: We are to stand against these lies.

That often looks like rejecting or in some cases ignoring the fear that the enemy presents to us saying, "The abandonment is going to happen again."

The enemy uses our past against us. And it's always him. People may look like the problem, but they aren't: the enemy is always the problem (see Ephesians 6:12).

This fear of abandonment comes from the broken world we all live in! But my favorite promise throughout Scripture is that our God (Jesus Christ Himself) will never leave us or forsake us.

We may be abandoned by our friends, our families, our communities, our churches, our boyfriends, our bosses, and even ourselves. But we will never be abandoned by our Heavenly Father, our Lord and Friend Jesus Christ. or our Counselor and Comforter, the Holy Spirit of God.

Never!

It is said in Psalm 118:6, *"The Lord is for me; I will not fear; What can man do to me?"*

The fear of being abandoned is a lie. It will tell you that you are something you are not; it will lie to you! It will say to you, "Be careful Lindsay, don't get too close. What if they leave you? You will surely die."

WHAT? SHUT UP, SATAN! I will not die!

The fear of abandonment is actually taking two lies and twisting them around each other to confuse us even more.

LIE #1: Fear
LIE #2: Abandonment

Change Your Mind

So what do we do?

I say, Google these promises and write them down on little white note cards and go over them every day for 40 days. This is called renewing your mind with the truth of the Creator of the Universe, God Himself.

Isaiah 35:4
Hebrews 13:6
Psalm 56:11
John 14:27
Joshua 1:9
Psalm 34:4
1 Peter 5:6-7
Psalm 56:4
2 Timothy 1:7

Romans 12:2 says:

"And do not be conformed to this world, but be transformed by the renewing of your mind, so that

you may prove what the will of God is, that which is good and acceptable and perfect."

Let's do what the Creator of the Universe says and be transformed by renewing our minds!

We are more than conquers in Christ. We are overcomers. We have Jesus on our side. WE WIN! End of story!

•   •   •

12

The Truth of Joy and Peace

Two things you can't fake are joy and peace.

"Joy looks above and not ahead. Joy is a deep-seeded assurance that He is in control and the admission that we are not," said my dear friend Sarah, a gifted Bible teacher who taught me the power of the Word of God and how to find Jesus in it.

When we lose our peace over something, it takes our joy right along with it. And peace and joy are the fruit of God's Spirit who lives inside of us, which we can access.

Our soul can lead our lives instead of our spirit. That is backwards. We must allow our spirits to lead our souls—the Spirit of God to lead our minds, wills, and emotions.

A few years ago, I was walking through a heartbreaking season that included my two biggest fears coming true within weeks of each other.

I would have my "control/protection/fear cycle meltdowns" quite often. Because of the pain, I would try to control outside circumstances that felt they might add to the pain I already thought was going to take me out. And then I would attempt to protect myself from anyone who could hurt me further—which, in my troubled mind, was basically everyone but God.

This led to fearing that, since God allowed the initial pain, maybe He would allow more pain I couldn't handle, and then I would die. I isolated myself because of fear, and felt alone, rejected and abandoned by everyone.

After a cycle would pass, I would see all the emotional energy I had just spent, and realize once again that God really does know the end from the beginning. He doesn't cause the pain, But He is in it with us.

I had to make a decision: was I going trust Him, or waste a ton of emotional energy freaking out when that didn't help anything? It often just made things worse.

As usual, He was kind to teach me the best way was to let go and to trust Him moment by moment. This seemed to be the theme of my life.

When I would grip a little too tightly again to something, He would gently remind me, "Lindsay, you can trust Me."

Fear causes the need for control—but as that season went on, He slowly showed me, moment by moment, that I could let go. He would help me.

When trauma happens in life, the lie of fear wants to come in and take over.

I have heard that in the Bible there are more than 365 times, in one form or another, that it suggests we "do not fear." And in my hardest season, I had to start internalizing those words, no matter what anyone else said. I had to believe His Word was the truest truth.

He is God; my friends and family aren't, my pastor isn't, my therapist isn't. I either believe He created the universe and can be trusted, or I don't. The Bible says:

> *"For a child will be born to us, a son will be given to us; And the government will rest on His shoulders; And His name will be called*

Wonderful Counselor, Mighty God, Eternal Father, Prince of Peace" (Isaiah 9:6).

Jesus says:

"Peace I leave with you; My peace I give to you; not as the world gives do I give to you. Do not let your heart be troubled, nor let it be fearful" (John 14:27).

When Jesus said, "Peace I leave with you," it seems He was referring to the Holy Spirit of God—who dwells within us, who is God, who is Jesus! It is Him, our Prince of Peace.

Therefore, invite Jesus not only into your life, but also into each and every situation. I invited Jesus into my life years ago. But I can often find myself living, thinking, and reacting to a situation as if Jesus is nowhere to be found. Reacting like Jesus has no idea what is happening and it's all up to me.

When I would finally humble myself and pray, asking God to help me, He did, every time. But I often found that He would allow me to struggle until I stopped and asked Him for help.

I needed to realize He is God and I am not.

Does Prayer Change Things?

Did the situation change after my prayer? No! The circumstances didn't change—but my heart did, my focus did and my feelings fell into place.

I have had to learn time and again to turn back to my Peace, back toward my Savior, King Jesus, and whisper in His ear, "I trust You."

Philippians 4:7 talks about the peace that surpasses all understanding. This is something I would often pray for all those around me who were in a season of suffering. As I faced my own valley, my own season of suffering, my own fear, I felt the kind of peace that truly does not make sense— when the circumstance doesn't change, but something inside of us does!

In my season of suffering, I struggled at first with wanting to sit in my fear, my sadness, my despair, my self-pity—like it was going to change something. It doesn't. Processing pain, yes. Wallowing in self-pity, no.

I lived without much peace or joy for most of my life. I wondered, "Why me?" in every trial and tribulation that came my way. But then I decided, "No more."

If it's truly up to me to let go and allow Jesus to be joy and peace in and through me, then I will—even if I slip up from time to time.

He promises He will walk with us; He will not leave us or forsake us! (See Isaiah 43:2, Psalm 23:4, Hebrews 13:5.)

Whether you believe in Jesus or not, you will endure suffering on this earth. But with Jesus, you can have peace.

Journal Moment

Father God, I need Your peace that surpasses all understanding in these situations in my life at this very moment.

Just list your situations out.

I find 1 Peter 5:6-7 to be so interesting, as it says to cast all our cares (some versions say all our *anxiety*) on Him because He cares for us. After that, it says to be of sober spirit and alert, because our adversary, the devil, prowls around like a roaring lion, seeking someone to devour.

I find it interesting that our worry, anxiety and fear seem to be an open door for the enemy to torment us, just as we discussed in Chapter 1.

So let's lay down our fears, our worries and anything that makes us anxious.

Prayer Pause

Father God,

Here is what makes me anxious, fearful and worried, but by faith I am laying this down at Your feet and trusting You will show me what I need to know or do. Thank You that the enemy cannot torment me when I lay my cares at Your feet, as You advise me to in Scripture.

You are God and I am not, so I am going to trust You even if my feelings want me to go a different way. I choose in this moment to trust You with all of the following.

In Jesus' name, I pray.

•   •   •

God helps us!

13

The Truth of Wisdom

He has all the wisdom!

Let us then approach God's throne of grace with confidence, so that we may receive mercy and find grace to help us in our time of need (see Hebrews 4:16.)

Paul, the writer of most of the New Testament, said, "Pray without ceasing."

Do you ever wonder what he meant there? Probably exactly what he said, "Pray without ceasing."

But what exactly does "ceasing" mean, I wondered?

So I looked it up. And *ceasing* means "to bring or come to an end."

It seems Paul was essentially saying, pray without stopping.

I know this sounds a little impossible.

But what I believe Paul was communicating is that there is never a bad time to pray. You can never pray too much or in the wrong way or in the wrong place. I find that I have a bit of time when going tinkle. Can we use that word? We are friends, right?

Whether I am at a party and in need some confidence, or at the office and in need of some wisdom, I can always shoot up a few prayers while in the ladies' room. Prayer is always effective no matter what the father of lies, wants to whisper in your ear about it being a waste of time or completely ridiculous. The devil is the father of lies and he is exactly that, a liar. Jesus made that rather clear.

As life gets crazy around us and we don't know what to do all of the time, we must lean into the One who has all the wisdom.

I know I have quoted from the book of James a lot already in this book, but I just can't get over the fact that God, who has all the wisdom, says we can come to Him and ask for wisdom whenever we need it. That's amazing.

"But if any of you lacks wisdom, let him ask of God, who gives to all generously and without reproach, and it will be given to him" (James 1:5).

I think it is no coincidence that this is written right after He talks about us all experiencing trials in life. Your trial could be bigger than you ever imagined or it might be tiny and seemingly insignificant.

The thing is, He didn't say come to Me only when your trial is too hard. He said if any of you lack wisdom, come ask of God, because He gives generously. It says He gives generously to all without finding fault. Meaning He is not mad at you that you don't know what to do. He is asking you to come to Him.

A-MAZ-ING.

He often has to remind me that the point of this life is to be in relationship with Him. It's hard to imagine because the world beats us up so much. But there is a God in heaven who wants to talk with us 24/7. He doesn't sleep and He literally has all the time in the world for you.

Yes, you.

He delights to be with you.

He doesn't care if you are on the potty or in the shower, washing dishes or crashing into bed. He just wants you to turn your affection toward Him, to ask Him in a five second prayer for what to do about this little tiny seemingly insignificant situation.

Right after James 1:5 He says: *"But he must ask in faith without any doubting, for the one who doubts is like the surf of the sea, driven and tossed by the wind"* (James 1:6).

Now I know the above sounds a little harsh. But sometimes we may have to ask Jesus to help our unbelief and that's okay. He is that good. He will help our unbelief, if we ask.

Your prayer may look like this:

Jesus, help my unbelief, I need your wisdom and I want to receive your wisdom on _____. In James, You say we can ask for wisdom and it will be given, so here I am, asking!

And watch what He does! It's so exciting to actually walk the moment by moment surrender and adventure with God.

Now let's get to walking with Him, moment by moment, seeking His wisdom in every single tiny thing we do.

•   •   •

14

The Truth of Identity

Why is identity so important?

Because "For as a man (woman) thinks within himself, so he is" (Proverbs 23:7).

What we believe about ourselves, deep down within our hearts, we will ultimately become.

I used to think really odd things about myself. But at the time, I thought those weird things *were* me. I didn't know I had a Creator who adored me. And I surely didn't know I had an adversary who wanted to destroy me.

I had no idea there was a war around me.

I didn't know I had a choice about where I found my identity. I thought that I was just who I was. "I must have been born this way," I would say.

That's what people told me That's what TV told me,. That's what my feelings told me. That is what *life* was telling me, and I didn't know I had a choice in the matter.

So I accepted it.

I didn't know Scripture said I would actually then become it.

This breaks my heart.

I spent so many years believing awful things about myself that I had to drink myself into oblivion to drown them. And then it turned out they weren't even true.

I don't pretend to know why other people take their own lives—but I remember wanting to take mine. It was because of the lies I believed about myself. And because I believed them, they felt true.

God desperately wanted me to know who I was, as His beloved daughter. But He gives us free will, so I got to choose what I believed.

I heard the thoughts in my head so clearly. They were so mean, but I didn't know I was being lied to. All I heard was:

You are worthless Lindsay, you are such an idiot,
I can't believe you thought anyone would ever love

you. Look what you did! You left everyone who would love you and now look at you. Pathetic. You might as well just call it quits, you are SUCH a loser, NO ONE WILL EVER LOVE YOU.

I didn't know the mean voice wasn't true. I believed the mean voice and it made me hate myself even more.

What Does Identity Mean?

The actual word *identity* means, "the fact of being who or what a person or thing is." That's deep. What a person is. What are we.

I think my sociology professor wrote that on the blackboard back in college.

What Are We?

- Are we who we love?
- Are we who we hate?
- Are we what we desire?
- Are we what we do?
- Are we what we feel?

According to the Bible, no. We are not what we do, not even close. We are, in fact, none of these things.

We are beloved children of the MOST HIGH GOD. Anything that tells you different, even if it seems like your own thoughts, is lying to you.

The lie that tries to tell us no one will ever love us is the furthest thing from the truth—because we are *already loved*.

So what do we do?

We ask.

What is God saying about me? And what is the enemy saying about me?

The only true and sure way to know this is to search Scripture to find out what the Creator of the Universe has to say about you. Because it is not only true—it's beautiful, it's stunning and it will make you blush!

You are not all those things the people around you say you are. You are not your feelings. You are definitely not those mean thoughts in your head. You are not what the media says you are. But you are without a doubt who GOD SAYS YOU ARE, and I can promise you that even if you don't *feel* like that, it doesn't mean it's not true.

If what you think about yourself doesn't line up with Scripture, you are being deceived. Let me tell you: I was deceived and I know the destruction that will slowly bring to your soul.

So when I tell you what you think you are may not be true, I am speaking from experience.

Has it taken time for me to unravel those lies? Yes, a long time, actually. But He is a Healer, a Restorer, and a Redeemer—and if we continue to seek Him, He will show us the way to the truth.

Prayer Pause

Father,

God I pray for these precious people that read this book. You know every hair on their heads. You know every desire of their hearts, and You know every lie they are believing about who they are.

Lord, reveal it. Send Your Holy Spirit to show them the truth of who they were made to be, who they are in You. Lord it's only by Your grace that any of us are free from the lies. Come and heal our minds, hearts, bodies and souls, our emotions, our wills. God, we can't do it without You.

•   •   •

15

The Delightful Truth

Years ago, a dear friend whom I immensely respect said, "Lindsay, let go and let God write the story of your life."

I honestly hadn't heard that before. I always thought it was up to me to make my life what it was going to be. I thought it was my fault if my life turned out to be a failure.

But as she said this to me, I had this image of literally giving a pencil to God every time I wanted to control the next "chapter" of my life, or even the next step, which was just about all the time. I would sense a tap on the shoulder reminding me to "hand the pencil back to God, Lindsay."

That became a mantra for me. "Put the pencil down, Lindsay," I would say to myself. I said it daily. Then I began to say it moment by moment—this fun, kind of silly reminder that giving all the little parts of my life to God would only benefit me in the end. I say *benefit* because well, He is God and I am not.

This 'thinking I was God' thing put a lot of pressure on me that I didn't handle well. Instead of walking with God, step by step, allowing His Spirit to guide me and His Word to be a lamp unto my feet, I stressed about every single decision like it was a matter of life or death, literally. I guess that's what you do when you think you are God. Oops.

Thankfully, by His grace and help, I learned (and am still learning) to walk with our Advocate, the Holy Spirit.

I learned how to stop and ask God to help me with the smallest of things. And He did. I will admit I was often surprised. *Why does God always help me find my keys?* I wondered.

I think I can say that most of us who struggle to trust God or receive His love do so because we don't think He cares about the tiny details of our lives.

It is often the smaller things in life that surprise me and make me wonder (in a good way) how God could be so real. The big things are always nice—marriage, children and fulfilling career—but to think a big God cares about my keys is fascinating to me. It's sometimes hard for me to compute, but I often notice when I am running around looking for my keys and I stop and ask Holy Spirit to help me, I find them. But when I just try to find them in my own strength and think, "God has more important things to do than help me with my keys," I find myself searching a lot longer. It's like He waits for me to ask.

As I was getting ready to go on an exciting 40th-birthday adventure with the Lord to Europe, I stopped in at the Hollywood House of Prayer, where I went from time to time to worship the Lord, receive ministry, and minister to others, too.

On this particular night, a visiting pastor was there, praying and prophesying for everyone. (Prophesying just means listening to what God is saying over different people.) I had never met this particular pastor, and didn't speak to him that night either. He didn't know my name, but He heard from God very clearly about my situation.

As the night came to a close, I sheepishly raised my hand to receive prayer. As this man who had no idea I was going anywhere started to pray, he said, "God is going to take you away for two to three months." (I was leaving in five days for what ended up being just over three months). He went on to say, "God is going to wrap you in a silk cocoon like a butterfly."

Let me take a moment to tell you how God has spoken to me through butterflies for the past six years.

I had never been a "butterfly person" before. Frankly, I thought nothing of them. That was until I heard my friend Larry call his wife, Jody, a butterfly.

Jody is one of those super-creative souls who is lovely in every way. When I heard Larry call his wife a butterfly, it was the most endearing thing, and it hit my heart in a real way.

He went on to say, "Jody just flies around from one thing to another, beautiful in all her ways."

My heart softened as I felt God nudge me and whisper, *That's you, too, Lindsay. That's who you are, that's how I see you.*

I lit up on the inside, but my head sunk down into my chest. Could that be true? All these years I thought I was just a mess of a person, so disorganized and not like everyone else. I thought this was a flaw in my personality. I didn't know it could be beautiful. I didn't know it was beautiful.

It was as if God came into my head and rearranged how I saw myself in a matter of moments. I had always thought something was wrong with me, but this exchange redefined how I saw myself. And in that moment, butterflies became very significant to me.

It was nearly outrageous how often people would pray for me and see butterflies in their mind's eye over me. I couldn't ignore this theme in my life. It was so encouraging.

It was as if all these years I thought my creativity was a flaw in my personality—but it was what made me *me*. I got a huge part of myself back that day.

The Father's love is so real. He will pursue your heart until you understand His deep love for you. And He will step over every wall you build up to show you His adoring love.

The Process of a Butterfly

Years later, God began to show me how a butterfly is in darkness in its caterpillar state for a long, long time before it becomes beautiful and able to fly. This resonated deeply with me because on the outside, most people thought I was doing just fine.

But on the inside, I lived in deep, deep darkness that no one really knew about.

Living in inner darkness, fearing something is deeply wrong with you, causes self-rejection and self-hatred. It forms lies that say "if anyone knew, they would not accept me or love me."

Unlike pain on the outside, there is no one there to cheer you up or champion you through. It's just you and your thoughts. And when those are influenced by the spirit of darkness, it leaves you feeling hopeless.

The healing isn't obvious either. No one knows you are going through surgery on the inside, because there are no doctors performing it.

It is the Holy Spirit who resides inside, He is the Doc. He is the One doing the work. And the work doesn't always come right after the pain—it can be decades later. Therefore, it can seem even more awkward to those around us. It can take a long time and be deeply personal, and all the while no one else is even aware of it. No one is helping you through your illness because no one knows you are ill.

So you cling to Jesus, because He is the only One who knows and truly understands. And the good news about that is He is the only One who can heal you anyway!

I have seen God internally heal people in many ways, inside and outside of marriage, in the midst of divorce and disease, through miracles, signs and wonders, doctors and medicine.

For me, it happened when life as I knew it came to a screeching halt.

God invited me to to leave my six-figure job and trust Him. What I thought would be a three-week break turned into a six-month sabbatical—and then three years of part-time work and part-time recovery. And just when I thought it was over, it got more intense! But at the same time, His blessings got more intense, too.

He blessed me beyond my wildest dreams during the most intense part of the healing process. He is such a kind Father. I lived in the most beautiful fairy tale of a home—one of those only-God-could-do-that kind of miracle stories.

The Lord had shown me that He was doing brain surgery and heart surgery on me at the same time. Which, as you can imagine, was painful—but He knew that beauty was very healing to me, So He gave me the most gorgeous place to live, in one of the most expensive cities in America.

For free.

Because He wanted me healed and whole more than anything else.

I was financially in a hole and had such guilt over my financial situation. But He said to me, "Lindsay, if you had cancer you would use whatever resources you had to get healing. No one thinks about this when it comes to emotional healing. I don't care if it costs a million dollars—I want you healed."

Which, as you can imagine, shut up the condemnation I felt about my financial situation.

And all of this happened after I thought my "season of healing" was over. I guess He was just getting started—on the deep, deep stuff, anyway.

Season of Healing

I would sit with God for hours and hours. I would cry for hours and hours, and felt as though this was never going to end, this "surgery" of sorts. I often thought I was crazy. *Is this* really *what He wants me to do?* I would think. But breakthrough after breakthrough, the fruit was obvious. I couldn't deny His work in my soul. It was worth every penny.

I asked Him one day what He wanted me to know. I would sometimes see these little stick-figure drawings in my mind after I prayed, and I would "sketch" them out in my journal (I use the word *sketch* lightly here, as I am the worst sketch artist ever). But one day, I saw a cave and a stick-figure Jesus standing outside. I asked God what it meant, and He gave me the notion that my heart was in the cave and He was on the outside inviting it to come out.

Weeks later, I dreamed of a room that looked a little bit like a jail cell with exposed brick walls (I love exposed bricks). I saw lace curtains going up. Then the scene changed to a beautiful home with all semi-white crown molding and a bustling fire in the gorgeous fireplace. Then God let me know that both scenes were my heart. And He was making it all new. He said I had been trying to "fix up" the jail cell heart with some lace curtains, but He was doing a full remodel.

I spent most days journaling, reading my Bible, crying or on my knees praying, or reading white index cards with truths written on them to combat the lies I believed. It was rather intense at times. But as I said, the blessings were intense too. Because He is a good Father.

I remember facing things that scared the daylights out of me. I remember having hard conversations that scared me so much I had to take walks for hours praying and almost forcing myself to believe the truth that God knew what He was doing, even though it felt so very painful.

You might have found me jumping up and down screaming the truth, ignoring the enemy as much as possible. (God knew I needed to live alone in this season!) I was typically pumping myself up as I would face one issue, and then another issue, and then another.

It was like I was jumping hurdles in a track meet, but with the kindest Coach ever. *You can do it, Lindsay*, He would write to me in my journal.

He is so nice.

God doesn't reveal what He doesn't want to heal. He was so faithful to be with me every single step of the way.

I tell you this to encourage you. Because we overcome the enemy by the blood of the Lamb and the word of our testimony. This is the testimony of His healing power and His divine kindness. He wants us whole and healed. But healing sometimes hurts.

But be encouraged: He will bring joy into your mourning and He will give you a garment of praise for heaviness.

I know this because He has done it for me—and what He does for one, He will do for all. So be encouraged. I share my heart with you because the

Bible says to whom much is given, much is required. I have been given such grace in my pain, and I want to offer that same grace to you.

Friends

One evening at church a friend who was practicing asking God for pictures to share with people in order to encourage them said, "Jesus, what do you have for Lindsay?"

He paused for a moment, then said, "I see a picture of a teddy bear that has been ripped open but is being sewn up with golden thread."

My friend didn't really know all I was going through, but he heard from God that night. I knew exactly what it represented, even though I could tell my friend wasn't sure it was helpful to me. As my eyes filled with tears, I knew it was God once again showing me that He was healing me—that He was not only sewing me up, but He was sewing me up with gold.

He was healing me with the best.

As I got further revelation about the vision my friend saw for me, I remembered being a little girl in and out of the hospital with all kinds of really odd issues. They would bring carts around filled with toys for you to choose from; I would often pick the stuffed animals. I am not sure if they were all teddy bears, but they were soft and snuggly for sure.

It was funny how thirty-five years later Father God would use something that I found comfort in as a child to bring me comfort in my current situation. He is way bigger and way kinder than we often realize.

If He would do little, seemingly silly things for me, He longs to do them for you. This is who He is. He is a personal, loving God. The Bible says he is LOVE. We must learn to let Him love us. I am not special and surely have not done anything to deserve His love. No one has, everyone has fallen short of the glory of God, all have sinned. It is Jesus who makes us all worthy of His love.

How I Found Freedom

I was tired of being trapped, but I knew the way out was to face it. So I just kept going and going after what had hurt me.

I put myself in the situations I feared most. I would think, *I can't, Lord. I can't. This hurts beyond anything I have felt before*, as I would watch the guy I liked flirt with another girl. It reminded me too much of my old wounds. It hurt. I would stumble into the bathroom and say, "I can't, Lord." And barely get out the word "Help!"

Oddly enough, I found myself out in the middle of the group praying for people minutes later. It was as if God plucked me right out of the bathroom and placed me back in the middle of the scenario that I thought I couldn't be in, and I was okay. He answers prayers like that all the time.

I used to believe God was busy with world wars and starving people. I didn't think He had time for my little, random issues in life. Although they seemed huge to me, I figured they were nothing compared to what others were dealing with.

This was the tape that would play over and over again in my mind—but the belief that God is limited like we are is simply not true.

The Mean Voice

Even after that day in my bedroom, crying hysterically, hearing that mean voice scream at me that I was worthless, disgusting and would never be loved.

It was Love Himself that had been waiting and knocking for a lifetime wanting me to open the door. To even say "God" was good enough for Him. To recognize that He was there, which started the journey towards Love Himself, the most perfect Heavenly Father I had never known.

It took time to realize that He really did care, just as in any relationship we have to learn and put forth effort. Not striving to please Him or earn His love, but rather effort to get to know Him—which, like any relationship, meant spending time with Him through His Word and His Spirit.

Gathering around His name, usually meant at church or in a fellowship environment to learn about Him and grow in my knowledge of who He was with other children of His. Serving with time, money and talent for His sake, learning to worship and surrender moment by moment.

I learned He has all the wisdom and He wants to help me through life. His Spirit who lives inside of us is called our "Helper" in the Bible (John 14:26). He did that for a reason. He wants to help us in everything. In all our ways we are to acknowledge Him and He will *direct our paths* (Proverbs 3:6).

He is big enough to be with each and every one of us step by step on each of our very unique paths. And He says He will *direct* them as we look to Him for guidance. I know we often want to zip by these scriptures shaking our heads, saying, "Yes, Lindsay, we know that one," but I wonder if we really do believe it with all of our hearts. I know I do sometimes and other times I don't.

I believe He wants us to know it all of the time, because knowing that brings peace and rest to our souls. I love to further understand what He might have been saying. I want to roll it around in my head and suck every morsel out of the Scripture.

So I looked up the word *direct* in the dictionary. I found a verb definition for the word that says: "aim (something) in a particular direction or at a particular person."

If I may suggest what God might be saying, it's that He is aiming us in a particular direction or at a particular person. Hmmmm … what could that apply to in your life right now?

Do I think He has a husband picked out for me? I don't know. I think He knows who I will end up with, because the Bible says that He knows everything.

Do I believe there is only one guy on this earth for me? Heck no! If that were true, someone would have messed that up a long time ago. But what about this idea of God "aiming us toward a particular person?"

Now, that is interesting.

Is that what Scripture is talking about? No, not particularly—but it is still a truth we can hold onto and apply in our lives. It's a promise that if we acknowledge Him in all our ways, He will direct our paths. Could that "path" be toward marriage? Could that "path" be toward a certain person? Maybe.

If we take this little bit of knowledge and think through it in our real lives, it is very interesting. It's deep and can bring some great revelation.

His Word is living and active. It's not like the words in this book, they matter for a moment. But the Bible is sharper than a two-edged sword.

God gives us free will. We can make all our choices in life, even the choice to choose Him. In a world where we want control, an all-sovereign, all-knowing Creator of everything gives up control to allow His children to decide. Yet He says if we lack wisdom, we can come to Him and ask. That's an amazing Father—fully in control but releasing control, right there available to us when we need wisdom.

Oh, praise You, God! You are so much better than we imagine. He says:

"Do not fear, for I am with you; Do not anxiously look about you, for I am your God. I will strengthen you, surely I will help you, Surely I will uphold you with My righteous right hand" (Isaiah 41:10).

He is available anytime to talk and listen. He is our Father. He could have referred to Himself as anything, but He choose to call Himself our Father. He knew we would all need a Perfect Father.

Why Worry?

When we worry, instead of looking to Jesus— instead of asking for peace, or for the next right step, or for Him to be tangibly present in the mess—we miss out on His amazing grace.

Worrying won't stop what we fear. It will only steal from our lives.

It is said that His grace is sufficient in our weakness (See 2 Corinthians 12:9).

After finding His grace, realizing the struggle and becoming expectant with our hearts, we learn the safest place to be is with Him moment by moment, giving it all back to the One who created us in the first place. It is said that He knit me together in my mother's womb (See Psalms 139:13). He is not only more capable of leading my life that I am, He is the Creator of it.

Like most of us, I just didn't know He cared.

Life can be crazy. It's like one miracle and miraculously answered prayer followed by a run-in with fear, worry and anxiety, tempting us to freak out. Asking the question "What if?" which only comes to hijack our peace, steal our joy and try to take us out.

But be encouraged.

In every situation we have a choice. Are we going to attempt to control it, work it out in our heads, manipulate it, make it happen? Or will we do the hard thing—which ends up being the best thing—which is to be still and know He is God?

•   •   •

16

How God
Crushed the Critic

In closing, I am going to tell you a story—a story that shows the redemption of God, a story that proves He is our Helper and He creates us to be overcomers in Him, Christ Jesus. This is not a story of a sudden miracle, although I have experienced my share of those and I pray you will, too.

This is a story of a long, slightly terrifying journey that ended in victory. Not everything I wanted all wrapped in a bow—not yet, anyway. But it proved the faithfulness of God, and almost seemed like a movie as I was walking through it.

He who started a good work in me will complete it. (See Philippians 1:6.)

As I have mentioned throughout this book, my main source of extreme anxiety, worry and depression was a deep fear of men. I allowed men to use me more times than I care to count.

Why?

Because I was broken. I was confused. I didn't know the Truth that came to set me free.

In my experience, God often tells us to step out in areas where we feel uncomfortable. I have found God is more interested in our healing than in having us get what we want when we want it. I know He doesn't set out to disappoint us. Rather, we let our expectations disappoint us by taking the pencil back and trying write the story the way we want it to happen.

And it's okay, we all do it. But from my stepping-out-of-the-boat moments that ended in a little bit of a swim, I realized it's best to let Him show me what He wants to show me rather than assume what He is doing.

While in England on my 40th birthday adventure, I knew God was going to get to the root of a few of my issues because when I was at the Hollywood House of Prayer, the man who told me about God wrapping me up in His silk cocoon also said that would happen, and it was going to hurt a little. He said I was going to have to die to a few things, but then said the reason he was telling me this was so I wouldn't think it was the devil.

So I was prepared, because I wanted to walk in the freedom Jesus died for.

While in London, I found myself really attracted to a particular man I met. He had all the qualities I want in a future husband, and I was building up the internal confidence to believe that he liked me, too. All the "signs" were there, so the story in my head went.

The truth is, for me to believe that a guy I found attractive might be interested in me was a foreign concept. See, when you have dealt with self-hatred as long as I did, you can't see why anyone else would like you, because you don't like yourself.

But God!

He was working behind the scenes, and I finally felt confident, after all these years. I knew this guy thought I was pretty.

I would see him every so often at an event we both attended, and I was sure he liked me. I was sitting in church one evening and felt the Lord remind me of how Ruth "presented herself to Boaz" by lying at his feet.

No, don't worry. I didn't go lie at this guy's feet. (But it would have really added to the story if I did!)

God kept laying this "presenting myself to a man" thing on my mind. I knew it was God because it sure wasn't me. The idea terrified me in an oddly peaceful kind of way.

I knew it was God, because the thought came to me with this exact phrasing, which is the last thing I would ever say to myself: *Present yourself to a man.* I mean, no thanks. You have got to be kidding me.

But then I heard in my head, *If you don't do it this time, you will just have to do it next time.*

With a deep breath, I realized I needed to ask more about next steps.

What was God talking about?

What exactly did He want me to do?

Not long afterward, little thoughts came to me about grabbing coffee with this guy. After checking with my super-wise and very conservative friend back in the U.S., who is all about the man pursuing the woman, she agreed that this seemed to be what I was supposed to do. These things can be risky, because no one hears from Holy Spirit clearly every time. But sometimes God asks us to risk.

I would even say, He *often* asks us to risk.

So, with fear and trembling, I mentioned it in an email in a very appropriate way to this guy.

I got no response for two days.

I told God, "Okay, I did what You said, and now I am done!" I was going to see this fella that night at our group gathering, and knew *my* God would *never* ask me to go to the same place this guy was going to be after he rejected me ... but I had a nudge that I needed to go.

"UGHHHHHHHH, how can you make me go?" I wailed.

After a slight meltdown, I knew for some reason this was exactly what God wanted me to do—go.

So off I went. At the end of our meeting, the guy approached me and said, "When do you want to go for coffee?"

I was surprised—and then I was ecstatic. But this is where I went wrong: I started to assume instead of just staying surrendered. I spent the next few days dreaming about what this could be, telling a few trusted friends and writing the *love* story a bit in my head.

Put the pencil down Lindsay, put the pencil down. I wish I had listened to that little whisper in my head, but no—I was just skipping down the streets of London, thinking about my upcoming wedding.

Yes, I know.

And as you might imagine, the coffee didn't go as I had hoped. And that brought deep disappointment, along with a screaming mean voice behind it saying, *Lindsay, ha! You really thought this guy would like you? You are so stupid; you are such a loser.*

No one will ever love you.

Twelve years of life and healing later, and that same lie was able to take me down and puncture my heart. But this time, only for a short moment. Now, I knew better. I knew not to take this rejection in and let it fester. I knew how to grieve my pain and then move forward.

Winning!

But, I still needed somewhere to go and process that pain. I needed to cry it out. One of the churches I frequented during my time in London was holding a worship night that evening—so I hustled my way over there once I "just so happened" to be reminded about it by a friend who had no idea what was going on in my life.

Thanks, God.

It couldn't have been more perfect. It was a dark, intimate atmosphere, I didn't know a soul, and the music was loud. I could cry all my pain away.

You may be thinking, "Really, Lindsay? You knew this guy for a month and you were that upset?" But our present circumstances, unless tragic, are usually hitting a bruise from an earlier time in life when the "root of rejection" or "root of unworthiness" or whatever your root is first came in, and then all the times pain was piled on top of it.

It's like a cut that scabs over, but keeps getting broken back open again and again. It's often more sensitive than the rest of your body to pain. It's the same with internal wounds like rejection or abandonment. The root issues the Lord wanted to heal were my fear of rejection and fear of unworthiness.

When something happens and our reaction to it doesn't quite line up with the situation, it probably means we are grieving an earlier pain that is still in the process of being healed.

We want husbands, or better marriages or jobs or dreams to come true—but God knows that healing our hearts will make everything else richer. He blesses us all along the journey. But He is the destination, and the healing of our souls is His goal.

After I cried it out—and I mean I cried for like an hour, *hard*—the ministry team called for people who needed healing in their hearts. I knew even though it wasn't physical healing, my heart needed mending. After all these years, I was just getting to the root of it all.

My heart was broken.

That night was powerful, because when little situations with men happened in the past, it took me years to get over them because I didn't know how to get out of the pain. But this time I knew I had to cry it out and then I could move on—and that is exactly what happened. I cried it out, hard, loud and not pretty. But who cares? It was out and I could move forward.

Trying Again

A few weeks later, I felt I needed to step out of the boat again. In the past "trying again" would have taken me months, but this time it only took weeks.

Winning!

I felt as though I was supposed to join Christian Connection, which is what the Brits use to meet other Christians in the online dating world. I didn't really want to, but I knew I just needed to keep taking steps forward in this journey out of fear and into trust with God in this area that had entangled me for decades. Men, marriage and dating.

So I set up a profile and went about chatting with guys for a few days. But since these sites need to make money, after a few days I couldn't email the guys back anymore. I could only send an automated response which went something like this: "I am not a member so I can't respond."

I didn't want to pay for it, so I just let it go.

Even when things seem illogical, I have found God has a reason for them.

I went on with my amazing journey through Europe, just being blessed by God in amazing ways. As my trip came to an end about a month later, I cried many tears learning things that only God knew I needed to learn, struggling through lies and learning to overcome, getting prayer when I needed it and sitting at the feet of Jesus learning to receive His love yet again.

My last Sunday in London, I decided to go back to Holy Trinity Brompton, a church that reminds me a lot of my home church in Los Angeles.

After stopping at a makeup store to try on some pink lipstick (which was rather tacky, to be honest), I strutted down the streets of Kensington, my dirty hair thrown up in a messy braid, and popped into the little coffee shop attached to the church.

I sat down and was talking to a lovely older woman when I noticed a guy sitting across the way. He had a euro style hat on and was totally engrossed in a book. I thought, "Hmmmm, he's cute." I couldn't really look away, which isn't all that normal for me. I was really drawn to him and his style. He just looked like my kind of guy.

But as I walked by him, I heard in my head, *He would never like you, Lindsay.*

And there again, my thoughts lined up with a lie. I muttered in my mind, *Yeah, he would never like me.*

After church that evening, I received a "request" on Facebook Messenger from someone who was not on my friends list. I opened the message and it said:

"Lindsay, I hope this doesn't make you uncomfortable, but I was wondering if you were at HTB this afternoon? If that was you, I will tell you the rest of the story."

In the past, I would have overanalyzed this and been super-weird about it, but I wanted to be different. Actually, who am I kidding? God had made me different! I tapped right onto his profile to see his picture.

It was the guy from the coffee shop with the hat and the book.

I tried to sound casual in my response. "Oh hey," I wrote. "I just looked at your picture and yes—I saw you. You had a hat on and you were reading a book."

Okay, so I left the part out about thinking he was super cute, but still this was a big deal for me to respond without trying to make myself not look too interested.

I mean, who was I kidding?

He then asked me how long I was in London and I said I was leaving Tuesday, which was less than forty-eight hours away.

"Noooooo!" he wrote back. "We must have coffee tomorrow."

And then he said, "Are you curious how I found you?"

Honestly, I hadn't even thought that far.

"Christian Connection," he wrote back. "I messaged you six weeks ago on Christian Connection, but you never messaged me back. I thought I recognized you when you walked in the coffee shop."

I paused. "Wait … what?"

He said he proceeded to find me on Facebook through a church group we both belonged to. He looked up my name from my Christian Connection profile.

In the past, I would have worried that maybe it was weird or creepy. But this time I wasn't worried at all. I thought it was crazy (in a good way), to be honest. He then told me he didn't speak English too well but I could talk to him in French or Italian. (Did I mention I love accents?)

It was funny. We had great banter (which for me and an attractive man was r-a-r-e, because I was always Weirdo McWeirderson). But not this time; I knew I had changed. It was a freaking miracle. He ended up asking to have coffee the next day.

Not only was that little thought in my head from the coffee shop a lie. You know, the one that said, "He would never like you, Lindsay." The opposite was true. He *did* like me, and God was going to crush this twelve-year-old lie for once and always!

Go, God!

The day before I returned to America, this nice guy and I went to coffee. He was so kind to tell me to choose the place and the time, so I picked a little café on the water in the park near my apartment.

I woke up and got ready. With my orange tulip umbrella in hand and puffy winter coat on, I confidently set out for the café. I thought I knew where it was, but wound up getting really lost and ended up being thirty minutes late, sweating and slightly out of breath, trying to hurry in the drizzle. There he was, standing outside the café in the rain, waiting for me to arrive. "Why didn't he go in?" I wondered. "It's raining out."

We had a nice time. I was surprised and proud of myself that I could just be myself.

Winning!

Even after our conversation when I went in the bathroom and realized I had a bit of mascara halfway down my eye, I didn't care. I wiped it off and went back out. This was a miracle.

1. I wasn't weird.

2. He was so kind and respectful and cute and smart (all these things I like).

3. I didn't care that I looked a little bit like a soggy bunny by the time we met.

He asked me what I was doing that evening. I already had a ticket to *Le Mis: The Musical.* He asked if I would mind if he joined me, and I responded confidently, "No not at all." (This was so unlike me. Go Jesus!) He then asked me to send him the info about where I was sitting so he could get a ticket near me, so I did.

That evening when we met at the theatre, he told me they had no tickets left—so he wasn't going in, but he would wait for me until after the show. I was like, what?

Why would he do that?

He then said, "Ask how long it is. I will wait for you and then help you get home."

I said, "I've been here for three months. I know how to get home."

He said, "Well maybe we can spend just like ten more minutes together."

I asked the gentleman at the door how long the musical was, and he told me it was three hours. I turned back to Coffee Shop Guy and said, "It's three hours. Please, you don't have to wait," as I was being ushered through the door of the theater.

But he said, "Yes, I will wait. I will be right here when you get out." I thought, *Is this guy crazy? Why would he do that?*

As I found my seat in the stunning old theater, I ended up sitting beside this couple, probably in their mid-fifties, who were on a date. I asked them how they met, and they said, "Online." I then for some reason started telling them about this guy who was waiting for me outside, and they both said, "How sweet is that?" I thought to myself, *Okay, so that is sweet, not creepy?*

A thought then suddenly popped into my head: a five-year-old memory of my friend Sarah telling me I needed to find a man who would sacrificially love me. I remember having no idea what she meant by those words. But I realized this guy was being very sacrificial with his time to wait three hours to hang out with me for ten more minutes.

As the show went on, I got tired. But then I realized if I stayed up all night, I could sleep on the plane and beat jetlag. So I got a cup of coffee at the intermission.

Toward the end of the show, I heard words that for some reason stood out to me: "And remember, the truth that once was spoken: to love another person is to see the face of God." My eyes began to tear up as I realized God was showing me something.

God knows I have spent a lifetime worried and fearful of being loved because I didn't want to be hurt. I thought self-protection seemed safe. In the past I would have been so worried that this guy wanted something from me, that he could never just like me for me. Which had often been a perceived reality in my life.

But I had a choice to make: was I going to allow that past reality to dictate my current behavior? Well, by God's amazing grace, not this time!

By God's grace, something had shifted.

As I sat in the very last row of this stunning British theatre on my last night in London, I knew it was God. I didn't really understand what was happening. I didn't know this was the root He was probably referring to three months earlier at the Hollywood House of Prayer, the root that He was going to get to. I didn't know it would happen less than eight hours before I left to go back to America.

But as I look back, God—without much help from me—switched my perspective from one of worry to one of trust. Trust that the fears in my head were not real, although for 40 years they felt so real I couldn't seem to overcome them.

In that moment God switched something and I didn't even realize it; it was so natural and it was long awaited. Letting go of the expectation of what might be and what might not be, letting go of the control that I held onto to "make sure I didn't get hurt"—which was also making sure I was never fully loved either.

Something inside me of changed and I just didn't over-think it. I left the theater and walked around the corner—and there was Coffee Shop Guy, just standing under a light pole, right where he said he would be.

It was as if I was in the middle of a romantic movie. The kind of movies I couldn't even stomach most of my life, because I didn't believe love was really real.

I hated fairy tales and I hated love stories.

But God!

We walked down the streets of London's theater district, with shops on one side and big red double-decker buses on the other, lights shining from every which way, just talking. It was as if I was watching a person I almost didn't recognize—but it was me, and I was free.

I was free from the worry of what this guy wanted from me, I was free from the fear of rejection, I was free from feeling not good enough, I was free from the mean voice in my head. I was free.

We stayed up and drank coffee. He rode home with me on a double-decker bus—and when we hugged and said goodbye, I could tell he wanted to kiss me. But he didn't. Though he might not have known why, I knew why and so did God.

Five hours before I boarded a plane back to America, God was sealing up the lie that had held me captive all my life: the lie that not only would men not like me for me, but that they just wanted something from me. The lie that said "he would never like you" when just the opposite was true, not only did this guy like me, he pursed me and treated me like a princess.

Wow.

Twelve years later, God crushed that lie in such an epic way. A story I will never forget and a freedom I will always remember.

And that sweet guy, although we may never meet again, he played a profound role in the story of my healing. I never would have had the insight or imagination to write that story. Never in a million years for a number of reasons, but God. He is more real than the air we breathe, He knows every single thing that has been done to us and everything we have done, and He forgives it all.

God is a redeemer and a restorer. That is who He is, and therefore that is what flows out of Him for every single pain we have ever experienced. If we will humble ourselves and seek His face, He will deliver us from all that entangles us. It may not be in our timing and it may not be in the way we think, but He is faithful and it is His goodness that we get what we don't deserve.

It may have taken decades for me to hand the pencil back over to Him, so He could finally write a beautiful story of love for me to see, but we did it. We did it together.

He used this precious man, who will one day be an amazing husband for an amazing lady, to give me an example of what my standard should be from that point forward. It was as if He were saying, "Lindsay, I have been with you. I know all you have been though in this life, but now I am showing you as a perfect Father what you deserve and it shall be nothing less than this."

As I sit here in Southern California writing this letter, this book, this story to you, I still well up a bit with tears, as the healing will never stop until Heaven. But if we can just allow Him to show us what He wants to show us, which will be different for each and every one of us—if we can be more aware of His love and His real presence in our life—I believe we will live the greatest adventure, love story and fairy tale with God that we could ever imagine.

And our imagination is such a vital part of this journey. We all like to imagine what could be when a story starts, but then we need to release that idea back to Him so He can shock our socks off.

Once I arrived back in LA, I sensed the Lord asking me to submit my imagination to Him. I didn't know why, but I did so, with a brief prayer.

That evening at an event, a guy I knew came to sit beside me. I started to wonder if maybe he liked me. As clear as day, I saw a faint but clear sketch-type image in my mind of Jesus holding a fishing pole and kindly saying, "Reel it back in, Lindsay, reel it back in."

He was referring to my God-given imagination that can straight up get me in trouble with my what if's, even in the good things.

That evening as my thoughts wanted to run away into the sunset of this story in my head, I literally had to make a reeling back motion with my hands as I was driving. Then I cracked up laughing. Jesus was so tender to teach me how to not set expectations that I would then try to control, because that would begin a spiral.

Moment by Moment

Surrender isn't a one-time act, it is a moment-by-moment decision to trust the One Who loves us most over and over and over again. And if we mess up, we get to choose again the very next moment.

We can either "keep the pencil" and write the ending, the next chapter, the next scene, ourselves. Or we can hand it all back to our Maker one thing at a time. We can talk with Him to learn what He wants us to learn in the moment, and receive His pure love.

I sometimes (more often than I care to admit) wonder:

"Can I really trust you God in _____ (insert your struggle of the moment)?"

And then I think, who else on earth could I possibly trust more?

He literally created the world.

It's not always easy to go against our logical minds and trust in a spiritual Father, an unknown realm, that we will never fully understand on earth. But He did create us and He did create the entire universe. He knows every hair on our heads. He loves us most.

God loves us when we are at "our best" in our faith and when we struggle to believe Him. So, the question still remains. Is there really, truly anyone better to trust?

Journal Moment

Is there anyone better to trust than the One who created the universe and everything in it? Honestly?

Final Prayer

Before we part, would you offer up one last prayer with me?

Father God,

You are God and I am not. Please forgive me for my mistrust of You from time to time. Please help me to trust You more, moment by moment. Help me to hear Your voice and not the voice of a stranger. Help me to receive Your love every day and understand how wide and how deep Your love truly is for me.

Quicken my spirit when I want to worry, remind me to pray instead. Thank You for calling me Your child. I know there is nothing better than being Your child. I am so thankful to be Your child!

Help me as I walk step by step with You, holding Your hand. Help me to trust that You know best and You will lead me as I walk.

Thank You for allowing me to ask you anything at any moment, You are awesome, mighty, powerful and amazing!

I love You!

•　　•　　•

About the Author

LINDSAY MORGAN SNYDER is a business owner, ministry student, novice fashion designer and avid entrepreneur. She considers herself a crazy creative living inside a business person's body. Lindsay has worked with top leaders in the leadership space and written for everybody from Hollywood to Homeless shelters. She moonlights as a ghostwriter for other authors and is addicted to the Joy of Jesus. She loves words. Speaking them and writing them. She holds a high value for laughing, being awkward so others laugh and seeing people learn to value themselves.

Visit us at:
www.LettingLoveInBook.com

For more visit:
www.LindsaySnyder.com

We'd love to hear from you!
Lindsay@lindsaysnyder.com

• • •

Thank you, Dear Reader!

It's my hope and prayer that you found this book to be a life-changing read.

If this book helped you in any way, I would love for you to go to my Amazon page and add a quick review. Your review can reach others who are struggling to find help, healing, and love.

In faith,
Lindsay Morgan Snyder

Made in the USA
Columbia, SC
23 November 2022

71994687R00096